Social Anxiety

By

Clark Brown

Table of Contents

Introduction

We all know the feeling of being nervous or uncomfortable in a social situation or setting. Maybe you've clammed up when meeting someone new or gotten sweaty palms before making a big presentation, or your stomach knotting and rumbling at the thought of doing anything or indulging in any task that involves interacting with people, or communicating. Public speaking or walking into a roomful of strangers isn't exactly thrilling for everybody, but most people can get through it.

If you have a social anxiety disorder, though, the stress of these situations is too much to handle. You might avoid all social contact because things that other people consider "normal" -- like making small talk and eye contact -- make you so uncomfortable. All aspects of your life, not just the social, could start to fall apart.

Social anxiety disorder (also known as social phobia) is one of the most common mental disorders we have. Like it is called, it is the anxiety that comes with social settings and situations. So if you have it, there's hope. The tough part is being able to ask for help. That is what this Book is set to achieve.

– To let you know that whatever you are going through, you are so not alone. There are millions of people suffering from the same social incapabilities and are socially handicapped.

– To let you know that it is no fault of yours. We are all wired differently, and that makes us unique in our own ways. We should embrace our identities but not let them stop us from doing things.

– To help you understand your weakness and turn them into strengths.

Many people with SAD have avoided talking to others for most of their lives. Even when they are finally able to control their anxiety, they will often have no idea how to start a conversation, read body language, or identify social cues.

Some tips may help. The aim is to teach you that communication is about more than just speaking. Like any new experience, there may be stress and the occasional gaffe when you first start, but you need to believe that these are normal. By merely being present, things will improve, sometimes invisibly, as you become more accustomed to social situations. I hope this book gives you all the help you need.

Chapter One

You're Closer Than You Think

The biggest challenge to overcoming social anxiety has the desire to do so, having the passion and drive to want to shake off and break through the shackles of social anxiety. In essence, you've already decided to begin your success story with the one simple gesture, you've taken by merely saying "Yes" to ending this problem of social anxiety.

Social anxiety is a wrecking disorder that uses your seclusion and inability against you. Social anxiety must have deprived you of a lot of Things, of a lot of people, networks and productive interactions. Social anxiety must have filled you with enough self-hate, enough self-doubt, self-loathing, anger and bitterness that is capable of drowning any man or woman, that is capable of sinking you into steady states of depression. But you are closer than you think, you are already there. You are a winner already, just for living through that shame, the anger and getting to this point, this point of deciding to want to put an end to this wrecking disorder called "Social Anxiety Disorder." You are already a winner.

After years of feeling the debilitating anxiety that social situations create, the awkwardness, blushing, itchiness and sweatiness of the body whenever you are in social settings, or whenever you are put on the spotlight, or whenever you are about to become proactive and step out, engage in interactions with people; that blanket of shame, that wrecking moment. It is easy to fall into a bit of passive negativity about people, life and anything outside of your immediate control. Or to let depression overwhelm you as you sit in your closet, in your room or your closed circle and sulk, or be bitter about your inabilities to control things, to interact and be free in reality. It's normal. You are not abnormal; what you are going through is entirely reasonable.

I mean, why on earth would you want to go out with friends when the mere thought of what that entails brings about discomfort and irritability to you, when the idea of talking or working with another human makes your armpit sweat and begin to itch. Sounds like a terrible situation, right?

So, it's correct that you wouldn't want to engage in social settings. And that you would deliberately decide to avoid interactions and communications which would make you uncomfortable.

There's nothing wrong with you for feeling this way. What's cool is, you're smart enough to know that there's a better way – one that allows you to participate in life, to interact with people, enjoy other people's space other than your own and enjoy it.

This book is like a manifesto, and like every manifesto, it is crafty and specially written and tailored to help and show you that better way. It is meant to open your eyes to better realities, to the beauty of other truths that social anxiety disorder has deprived you of visiting and indulging in. The step by step exercises, philosophies, and strategies within this very great book will lead and guide you to a mindset and temperament that handles social situations exponentially better.

This system takes the fear out of social settings and puts you in the driver's seat. It shows you how to be in your element and control the flow of conversations; it brings you tips that help you understand the working of social settings. You steer the direction of your perception, and that is where the power lives, in your head. You can change how you feel at any moment.

This guide shows you how. It guides you through it all, like a mother grabbing the hand of a child and walking you through the processes.

So, the hard part is over. You've already made the conscious decision to go ahead and get over your social anxiety, which is the first step, the beginning of your victories. Now all that is left is to read this manual, watch the videos that are prescribed and put the knowledge that is given to use – that's all. You need to do it – and

you've already begun.

So, let's start by taking some of the immediate pain out of different social dynamics. Let's begin by going over how to deal with social rejection. Let's start by making the social setting seem less cumbersome; let's take away the shark teeth you see in social settings and demystify social settings for you.

Chapter Two

Dealing With Rejection

Rejection is almost unavoidable as a human going through life. There's no human being who has succeeded in love or life without first going through rejection. We all experience it, and it makes us feel very alone, outcast and unwanted. When you analyze rejection, you'll find out that most of the hurt and struggle we endure isn't even based on the loss itself but in what we tell ourselves about the experience. The ways we put ourselves down or surround ourselves with hopeless thoughts about the future is what makes rejection to ruin us.

Using and having the correct mindset and perception is essential when it comes to the issue of dealing with rejection in social situations. That's because, without the right approach towards denial, your brain will be consumed with fear, then anger and you lose your composure. The way you perceive a thing and understand it would go a long way in defining how you would interpret it and how you would go about reacting to it.

Sometimes, it could be the fear that the other person won't find you attractive, funny or remotely interesting enough. You may fear that you'll do something awkward or silly which will turn the other person off. You may even be afraid of future rejection - for example, maybe the initial social situation goes well, but down the road, the other person doesn't want to continue a relationship with you even after your first (seemingly) positive interaction.

These are just a few of the endless scenarios that your mind may conjure up when we talk about the FEAR of being rejected in a social setting. But this shouldn't be so. Rejection doesn't say you are flawed, or wrong or not good enough. You have to see it as rejection, they don't want you, and this had nothing to do with you. It is just their choice, and everyone is like that. I understand how much rejection eats deep into a person and wrecks their resolve and confidence, but if we can culture our mind to a positive way of looking at rejection, then we can interpret it better and maybe, just maybe, denial won't deflate our confidence when it does come.

But In reality, the rejection should be the least of your worries. It's that fear that's the REAL problem. That fear is crippling in many ways – 3 ways, specifically.

Fear Takes You Out of the Game

Fear is the opposite of faith. Fear is what comes before you get into an actor take action, fear sneaks into your joints, and while faith would push you and encourage you, and show you the strong points and advantages of doing a thing, fear would dissuade you, it would weaken you and give you every gory detail and embarrassing reason to not do anything. Every time you submit yourself to the fear of rejection, you unknowingly enforce that fear and make it stronger. The fear of rejection puts you out of the game; it makes you run away from stepping out to initiate contact. It sings all the tragedies of rejection, mystifies the scenario before you, and makes sure you slither back into your cave rather than step out and do a thing. Eventually, you become hypersensitive to social situations and settings that don't even warrant the anxiety being triggered inside of you.

And, I'm not talking about poignant moments in life like a first date or a job

interview, I'm just talking about socializing with friends at a casual gathering.

When that fear of rejection gets reinforced, after a while it grows so strong that the anxiety it induces becomes an automatic response to social situations. Walking up to a person or being approached, talking to a person or playing the audience.

The result?

You avoid social interaction and isolate yourself, then you create a haven for yourself and slowly begin to bolster the reasons why you are better off alone, further solidifying your social anxiety and the fear that fuels it. It sounds like an unbreakable cycle doesn't it?

Well, don't worry – I'll show you how to change that shortly. Bear with me for just a moment here because it's essential you understand your enemy – this ever debilitating fear.

Fear Sabotages Your Confidence

The second way that fear acts in holding you back from doing things and initiating contact is by sabotaging your confidence. As adrenaline pumps through your veins in social situations rather than make you rise above your regular wits, it would turn to a shock response. The same adrenaline rush that is supposed to heighten your senses and uplift your mood and fill you with witty ways to go about your interaction now becomes that force that blocks you. It begins to scream flight or run, and to see that your body is linked to your mind, your body begins to react negatively, filling you with discomfort and further pushing you away. This fear will restrict the authentic you that will attract others.

It dulls your personality in many ways because you'll be too self-conscious to enjoy yourself and that will feed into your conversations by giving others an unspoken, uneasy feeling. The fear picks out and heightens the features that repel it, and it shines a light on it. The flow of social interaction is interrupted by awkwardness that's hard for either party to explain. The low self-esteem you emit will make hang out there and be a looming deterrent to your otherwise good nature, and further act as a repellant between and others.

Fear Generates Defensive Hostility

Finally and perhaps most damaging, fear of rejection can frequently create a habit of defensive hostility. Because you're so worried about being rejected, you may come into the practice of denying others before they have the chance to hurt you. Fear makes you create a barrier around yourself and forces you deeper into your shell. Fear makes you spooky and overly cautious of things and scenarios you shouldn't be jumpy about.

Although it isn't a universal truth, if you get rejected enough and process that rejection in an unhealthy way, it can condition you to push others away preemptively or, instinctively feel negative about others for no legitimate reason.

Unfortunately, this habit causes you to lose even more self-esteem because the reality is, you know you're wrong for making these unreasonable judgments on others before you also get to know them. Fear makes you a horrible person and causes you to kick out others even when they are not close enough yet.

Try not to be too hard on yourself if you're guilty of having defensive hostility. The truth is, your mind is trying to protect itself from the anxiety of rejection. It may be going about it in the wrong way but – you're not a bad person for feeling this way. It is just the fear, and you have to acknowledge that and begin to make conscious decisions and take constructive actions to fight against it. You have to start rebuilding your confidence and self-esteem in yourself.

How to Interpret Rejection

Okay, so now that we've gotten all that ugly stuff out of the way, now we have handled all the repealing sides – I'm going to show you why rejection is a powerful ally to both your personal development and your ability to form unusual, fulfilling social connections.

Quick though, before I get into my super positive spin on rejection, I want you to do me a favor.

I want you to get away from the thought process of *"What's wrong with me?"*.

What is wrong with you, is the wrong question to ask, and the wrong way to perceive rejection. Most times when you get rejected, you may immediately begin to internalize the loss and turn on yourself - thinking things like.

"What did I say?" "What did I do wrong?"

"Is there something wrong with me?"

"Am I not good enough?"

"That guy that got accepted, in what way is he better than me?"

It is like putting your car in reverse when the destination you're trying to reach is right in front of you. You need to figuratively switch gears and change the way you immediately react to the rejection.

When you point fingers at yourself, nothing will ever be resolved or improved in terms of social anxiety. You need to embrace yourself. Every flaw, every faux pas should be celebrated and instantly forgiven. Then and only then can you move forward, only then can you embrace yourself and see rejection from less harmful and damning light.

Spending time torturing yourself after a social rejection will only make things worse so if you catch yourself playing the victim – interrupt the thought and focus on the next bits of philosophy.

Philosophy of Rejection

In life, in social situations, some people will resonate with you and some people will not. You cannot please everyone. Pleasing everyone should never be your goal – it's counter-productive. The fact that you were rejected doesn't speak ill or sour of you; in fact, it had nothing to do with you; it is just about the other person. Everyone has their own choices and preference, and you should tailor your mind to understanding that their options are not universally the best, it is just their choices.

That's because when you adapt your personality too sharply to fit into the paradigm of someone else's character, you rob yourself of your integrity. You become a shadow of who you are and should be. And this goes ahead to steal you of your uniqueness and take away that new bit and color that makes you who you are and should serve as your most attractive feature.

You change who you are.
That action alone takes away from your authenticity, and it's a move that is unsustainable in the long-term.

So, do not fool yourself into thinking that everyone can and should love you. It is not feasible; it is not even ideal for everyone to love you. Those who would like you would do so knowing who you indeed are and for who you are. Talk about loving unconditionally, because you are you. And those who wouldn't, those who would reject you, well, these people don't matter. And it is no fault of yours.

The Risk and Reward of Rejection

When you put yourself "out there" in a social setting, it may feel like you're putting yourself in a vulnerable place. Sometimes it feels safer to stay indoors and in your comfort zone and enjoy your space, rather than stepping out and exposing yourself to public opinion, to people of dissenting views and characters. After all, aren't you putting your pride on the line, your ego even?

Once you change your mindset and realize that there is nothing to lose, it becomes easier and more comfortable to suppress the fear of rejection. You begin to become more outgoing and more challenging.

Why do I say there's nothing to lose?

Well, think about it. If you get rejected in a social setting, you're still better off than if you would have done nothing. The outcomes are not conscious. That's because you gain experience AND you're participating in life which subconsciously reinforces your confidence. You get to understand better how to approach people. When you lose, you learn, and you try again, better than the last time.

Whether you get rejected in a social situation or not, you're facing your fear and conquering it. You are getting bolder; you are building a stronger self. Focusing on that fact alone will make diving into a social gathering easier because it becomes an exercise for your self-esteem.

Social success is a numbers game. Yes, you can align yourself with the right groups and increase the probability of acceptance, but ultimately everyone has a social circle. It's just a matter of trial and error to find the one that fits.

The tricky part is moving on after being rejected and putting yourself into the next social situation.

But, once you understand that it only wasn't meant to be, you take the onus or failure off of your shoulders and give yourself the strength to confidently move on. You learn to highlight and dwell on the good ones, on the lessons, and the small victories.

It's your world, no one else's. So navigate yourself towards people who love you and don't settle for anything less. After all, you deserve the love that you're seeking. You deserve to see, to be heard, to be loved and acknowledged. Just go out there, play the numbers game and don't stop till you find your social success. You are on the right track already, take charge of your life.

How to deal with rejection
1. Acknowledge Your Emotions

Instead of suppressing, ignoring, or denying the pain of rejection, you should acknowledge your emotions. Admit that it makes you embarrassed, sad, disappointed, or discouraged. Have confidence in your ability to cope with uncomfortable feelings head-on unfortunate this is essential to dealing with the discomfort healthily.

No matter what has caused the rejection, whether you were turned down for a job or promotion or you were stood up by a date, rejection stings like a scorpion bite. If you try to minimize the pain by convincing yourself or anyone around you that it was 'no big deal', then your grief will only be prolonged. The most efficient way if dealing with uncomfortable emotions is to face them head-on.

2. See Rejection As Pushing The Limits

Rejection serves as excellent proof that you're living life to the fullest. Whenever you're making a move, expect to be rejected, and it will make you unafraid to go for it.

If as a human you never get rejected, it may mean that you're living too far inside your comfort zone. You will not be sure that you're pushing yourself to your limits until you get turned down time and time again.

When you get rejected for a particular thing, you'll be self-aware and know that you're putting yourself out in the world.

3. Treat yourself with compassion

When you get rejected, do not berate yourself and tell yourself that you're stupid for making the step. Treat yourself with kindness. When you give yourself negative self-talk, respond with a kinder, more affirming message.

No matter what happened to make you rejected, beating yourself up will only let you stay down. Talk to yourself like a trusted friend. Swallow your harsh inner criticism by repeating mantras that will keep you mentally healthy.

4. Never let the rejection define you

As a person seeking improvement, try not to make sweeping generalizations when you're rejected. If you're turned down for a job, don't go ahead and declare yourself incompetent. If a lover denies your love interest, don't conclude that you're unlovable.

Do not let one single incident or one person's opinion to define who you are. You should increase your self-worth and don't make it be based on dependent on other people's opinion of you.

5. Learn From Your rejection

So you faced rejection, and you are feeling down, lighten up. Ask yourself, 'what did I gain from this situation?' It will help you evaluate and know what you learned from the rejection. Instead of only tolerating the pain, why not turn it into an opportunity for self-growth. With each denial, you should grow stronger and become better.

Rejection can be a good teacher. You may learn about areas in your life that need to be improved upon, or you may surprisingly learn that being turned down is not as awful as is imagined. Take advantage of rejection and use it as an opportunity to move forward with more wisdom.

Chapter Three

Stop Worrying About What Other People Think

When social anxiety is at it's worst, it becomes all consuming. It could sink you into depths of depression; it could handicap you and force you to either in your shells. It may even overflow into parts of your life that aren't social at all. You could begin to doubt yourself in every sphere of life, academically, even at work scenes. For me, I would feel a sense of paranoia sweep over me like an inescapable blanket. I begin to fear that there is a looming embarrassment about to happen, that something about would happen every time. It is a cage. You keep fidgeting and asking these questions that further pulls you down. In our society today, it is straightforward to get caught up in thinking about what people think about us.

What do people think about me? How are they judging me? Am I fairing well in their eyes? Are they talking negatively about me?

You may not even realize that you're fretting too much. Matter of factly, you may do that so consistently that you may not even recognize the signs of fear because it has become a part of you. These are some of the signs that indicate that you worry too much.

1. You're too afraid to talk to others about what you think or believe.

2. If you always think that people around you are upset with you when they aren't.

3. When you do things that you did not plan for it intends to do and still regret it afterward.

4. If you find it challenging to do something different and maybe even afraid to do so.

5. When you actively avoid certain people, mainly because you are scared that they don't like.

6. You only do what others tell you to do and find it very difficult to make your own decisions.

This damaging self-reflection can lead to nowhere good. So, apply the following strategies to end the anxiety of worrying about what other people think of you. Quit worrying about other people's perception of you and channel that energy into loving yourself more, seeing yourself for who you are and being content with you.

Now that you know the signs of worrying too much, you should stay working to save yourself. It's easier than you realize. The moment you understand and begin to incorporate these eleven (11) philosophies and strategies into your mindset.

Prioritize Your Passion

Take the time to ask yourself what matters to you in life. Sit and ask yourself what the things that matter most to you are, what are the things that make you happy. In what items do you find happiness and fulfillment. What would you want to define your life? Then figure out what you're compromising to fit into someone else's value system. Weigh your passion against the compromises and sacrifices you are making as against your passion and identity so that you can fit into other people's scope of interest.

Once you know your values and what drives you – your passion, your interests, your goals and abilities you'll feel more confident about your everyday actions. Understanding yourself very well will help you be more in your element, and more deliberate, more intentional in your decisions. That's because everything you say and do will be backed by purpose.

For example, you could say "I strive to be a great father, have a successful career, be a moral and generous person, etc." Use goals to initially define your passion lay out goals that would help you achieve your love and then expand your vision to form a complete picture of who you are or who you want to be.

When you feel confident about what you value and what you prioritize, you'll instinctively put those values above someone else's negative opinions.

It's Not All About You
The truth is, most people are anxious about themselves, not you. Most people's outbursts and treatment of others are just an extension of how they feel about themselves. Think about it, when you walk into a crowded room or a

public social setting, aren't you primarily focused on your actions and well-being? The way you react and respond to other people, is it not an extension of how you feel within yourself?

Well, pretty much everyone else has that same way of thinking. Everyone is internalizing their self while in a social setting and using it to affect other people too. They're not analyzing you under a microscope. If anything, they're more concerned with what's happening to them, with them and how you and everyone else see and perceive them.

I'm not trying to take you down a peg by breaking this news to you. But you're not as much in the limelight as you may think. Imagine walking down the road; I bet you imagine everyone else looking at you, watching your steps and how you carry yourself. You believe everyone is holding a microscope against you and watching you in every detail. But it is not so. Life is not so. You are barely noticed.

In some ways, this gives you the upper hand because you know people are concerned primarily with themselves and you can play to that to better orchestrate a positive, fulfilling social dynamic — more on that in a bit.

Sticks and Stones May Break My Bones.

Remember that nursery rhyme you learned as a kid that said, "Sticks and stones may break my bones, but words can never hurt me"? Well, it still holds as an adult.

Negative opinions about you can't hurt you unless you digest them, mull over them and let them hurt you. You have to permit those opinions to hurt you as strange as that may sound. You have to give these opinions the audience and stage to grow and bear down on you. Now, from time to time, it's possible people may have negative views about you for whatever reason best known to them. You should know that those opinions come from one of two places.

Either the person on the other side is insecure about their self and is throwing out negativity as a defensive mechanism or, the opinion is valid.

If there is some validity to the opinion, try to take the information and treat it objectively. Decide for yourself if the view is valid, or just the tantrum of a troubled individual. Don't just take anything someone says to you or about you as the truth. Process what was said and determine if it's worth your consideration.

Remember, you have the power to let words and opinions affect you. Choose to keep all feedback as constructive or dismiss it as a problem that rests with the other party involved.

Letting Go

You can't control what other people think, and in this light, your mantra needs to be "You can't worry about what you can't control." And let go of the things you can't control, let go of the things that are above your abilities.

If you do worry about what you can't control, you're going to instantly increase your anxiety by exposing yourself to a factor that's bound to sting sooner or later. You would keep yourself stagnant and immobile, unproductive.

It's crucial that you understand most social judgment, finger pointing and criticism comes from a place of insecurity on the part of the accuser.

Leave it at that and let the negative opinion be their problem, not yours. Carry yourself with high esteem and walk away from unconstructive criticisms that are coming from a place of insecurities.

You need to move on and focus on the positive, focus on your values and find comfort in knowing that you act in a way that's aligned with your belief system. And feel safe with the realization that you know where you are going, and it is where you want to go. Embrace yourself and let go of everything else.

Look More Outward

Internalizing your judgment makes you your own worst critic. All social anxiety is just your own internalized perception. You look at your actions with such granular detail that you pick apart every little thing that in reality goes unnoticed by those around you. Cut it out! Try to look more outward at what you want, expect and value rather than falling into the habit of internalizing and drawing inward. It will help you be more active in the social setting around you and allow you to leave your inhibitions behind.

Think About Why You Care

Many times, we worry too much because of what our social norms have inculcated in us. In this our time, we are being instructed to dress a certain way, act a certain way and even live a certain way. The popular belief of individuals is that anything that strays away from the 'norm' is too different.

Because of this belief, it can make us start to worry and

develop a fear of being judged by others. What you should do is try to recognize what makes you care and what you should care about so you can understand it better.

When you know that it is not your fault and that nothing is wrong with you, you'll understand that the society we live in has a role to play in the developed fear of rejection or judgment. Once you recognize this, you'll find it easier to start accepting yourself.

Be focused on being in the moment

It is always easier to stop worrying about things and focus on what's happening now when you are living in the present. Instead of thinking 'I like this outfit, and it looks lovely on me, what if people judge me for wearing it?', you would be thinking 'I love this dress and it's awesome'.

You will not focus your energy on what might happen because it is something you will be able to control. Try to channel your energy on the moment and accept yourself for who you are. Refrain from bothering about the 'could' and 'ifs' of the future. Once you do all this, it will be very much more comfortable to stop worrying about anybody judging you.

Know That People Don't Normally Care

All through our lives, most of the time, our focus is only on ourselves. This scenario is typical for everyone, including those people who you believe must be judging you. People go through life worrying about what others think when those people my boy be judging you or anyone else. Make efforts to realize that everyone has their own lives and the things try to have to deal with. Their thinking will be about themselves and not other people.

When you leave your house, you may worry that people will judge you based on how you're dressed or how you act. It may surprise you, but mostly everyone is thinking the same thing. A lot of us do not reply with plenty of thoughts about what others are wearing or doing.

Once you realize that other people have their insecurities and worries, it will be easier for you to stop worrying so much about what people think.

Practice Self Love And Acceptance

An essential thing to remember when we talk about worrying too much is that you have to love yourself first before anything else. Constantly worrying about what others think of you can show that you have little self-confidence and low self-esteem.

When you practice self-care for yourself by showing self-love, you'll not worry too much about what others think. Self-care can be done through meditation, spending time with nature, eating healthy, etc. Whatever it is that will bring you joy is enough, but make sure you show yourself you love every day.

Although it may take a while when you perfect the act of loving yourself, you can stop worrying so much and accept yourself for who you are. That way you don't need anyone's approval.

Find Your Group of People

No matter how severe your social anxiety is, there are still people with whom you relate very well.

When you are around those people who lift you and help you feel positive, it can help you to stop worrying about others. People who care about you will be able to emphasize your strengths and the positive things about you that you may not know. This intervention can help you on your path to self-acceptance.

When you have a close group of friends who are positive and honest, it will help because you can ask them questions whenever you feel like others may judge you and they will be truthful and accurate.

When you talk to your friends about your worry, they will point out the good in you and help you to start feeling more confident in yourself.

Understand That You Can't Please Everyone

Whatever decision or action you take in this life, one thing you should bear in mind is that you cannot please everyone. It is an impossible task.

There will be people who are always going to be judgemental towards you. It's just how they are wired. Even if people do judge you for something, they mostly never act on it or react by confronting you. It's just a thought that pops up in their head.

People who matter to you will probably never judge you while those who decide you may not matter. The earlier you accept the fact that you can't please everyone and that people will judge you no matter what, especially if that's their character, you will receive it and work on not worrying much.

Chapter Four

Conversational Confidence

Having an engaging, fun conversation with someone can sometimes feel like an intimidating endeavor. Socially Anxious people can find it difficult to express themselves in public and social settings, in places and scenarios that call for social abilities. Most people with social anxiety disorders are laden with social interaction and performance difficulties and hence, cannot perform and do tasks that involve other people. When you start to think about the technicalities of a conversation, it becomes especially challenging to relax and go with the flow.

Like Joshua, my high school friend who prefers his own remote space, his company over those of other people, people with social anxiety disorders find it hard starting a conversation, or know how to carry themselves around other people.

What do you talk about? How do you keep the other

person engaged? How do you make the conversation a "success" by definition of a good time?

I know breaking down a conversation on such a granular level might sound strange. But, if you suffer from social anxiety as I did, these details begin to complicate the fears of meeting people and getting yourself out there.

Here I am going to be giving you my seven (7) rock reliable tactics for conversational confidence. These are your go-to tools to help you navigate a conversation into a fun, enjoyable, anxiety-free experience.

After applying these tips to your everyday life and social interactions, you're going to look forward to meeting people and engaging them because these tactics steer the direction and flow of conversation, giving you control and putting both you and the other party at ease. Here we go.

Tactics for Conversational Confidence

Remember, these tactics apply to any and every situation. You could be on a date, at a party with friends, at an interview – it doesn't matter. These are tools for solidifying a positive social dynamic with one or many other people in all social settings.

1. Ask Questions

I've started this list with one of my favorite tips. Questions steer the direction of the conversation and allow the recipient to talk about what they most enjoy – themselves.

Everyone has an inner monologue running through their head all day, and the majority of people would love nothing more than an outlet to share these thoughts.

By asking questions, you show the other person that you care about them and have enough respect for them to give them "the stage" for a bit.

Asking questions also takes the pressure off of you to find something of mutual interest to discuss. You won't have to worry about inventing a topic that is pleasing for the other party because they will provide the content by answering your questions.

This method works wonderfully in all types of social situations, but dating is a particularly good example where questions are golden. When you're particularly unfamiliar with the other party in the conversation, questions are a great way to connect and bond.

Follow up questions are even better because they allow you to emphasize the good in the other person. So if the person answers one of your questions with something positive about them, you can follow up with questions that expand on the topic you already know they are proud of.

Questions provide a stealthy way for you to influence others by showing your genuine concern for their well-being.

2. Listen

One of the most important and most relevant techniques to bring a good conversationalist and to hold functional interactions with people is by being an equally great listener. The act of listening is fundamental, it makes the other person feel comfortable with you, and it presents you as an exciting person. Always have the golden rule by your side. "Treat others how you want to be treated."

You want to be listened to, then listen to others. Pay attention to them talk. Be friendly, be respectful. Look people in the eye as they talk, it shows you find them interesting, and you are flowing with what they are saying. When you are a good listener, people will notice and be more at ease with you. They would talk more and vibe with you. Smile as they talk. Follow their eyes. Insert appropriate words when necessary so that they will know you are interested in their conversation.

3. Give Genuine Compliments

That tip brings us to your next tactic, giving genuine compliments. Compliments are high, and everyone loves to get them. But, if you're complimenting someone just for the sake of making them feel good, it can seem transparent and desperate.

Opportunities to provide genuine compliments will arise all the time in social situations. Make sure only to give them out when you genuinely mean them.

Compliments work particularly well because they immediately disarm the other party and prove that your self-esteem is high enough to give credit to another person's strengths.

Are you starting to find a common theme with these strategies? They focus on directing your attention positively outward.

4. Verify.

Use the verification techniques to create great

conversation. This serves two purposes; First, it helps you to fully understand what is being said, verifying what you just heard, or what you think. Secondly, it shows you are vested and interested in the conversation. Verify. Use words Like "Really?" "When did this happen," "Please explain." It gets people talking more, and it helps you settle and be more comfortable and more in control.

Do well to ask open-ended questions. Open-ended questions are questions that you cannot answer with one-liners. Open questions help in keeping the conversation going and insist on indulgence. Open-ended questions begin with the five "W"s. Who, What, Where, When and Why? There is also "How?"

Here are a few examples.

– A close-ended Question: Are you a fan of rap music?

A close-ended question: What kind of two music are your favorite?

2. Look for the Good Values in Others

If you're having trouble providing genuine compliments to others, it's possible you have some insecurities of your own that prevent you from giving credit where credit is due. I'm not trying to provide you with a label here; this scenario is only a possibility. However, it's a fact that everyone and I do mean everyone has positive qualities that can be admired.

Widening your vision of what is beautiful and uniquely wonderful will allow you to be more in awe with the world and people around you.

I know personally, when my social anxiety was at its worst, I felt very cynical and jealous of people who could navigate social circles with great ease. I'd sit in my corner and begin to envy while I look at others connecting with people, sharing in laughter and bonding. Soon, I found negative excuses and reasons to stay on my own. It only fostered my seclusion and pushed me deeper into a recluse social setting.

Once, I learned to be more grateful for the world around me; I saw the harmony that all personalities bring to the table. And that allowed me to find ethical values in all people on some or many levels. You can do it too. You have to work on being more grateful for this one, a flash in the pan, a life that we've been granted and realize that every moment spent in this existence is a miracle. Sounds out there, I know. But nothing is more authentic.

3.Smile

Much like giving compliments, smiling disarms the other parties in the social setting. It simultaneously boosts your self esteem at the moment.

Smiling in a social setting is like wearing the appropriate attire for a special night out. Your smile is an accessory in social situations that you shouldn't be without. A smile makes you look confident, unbothered and like the perfect clothing, it attracts people to you.

Now, I know that when social anxiety makes you feel awkward, it's challenging to find your smile. You may be uncomfortable in your skin. That's why following

the self-esteem building lessons I'm going to be giving you, later on, will back up that smile.

A smile should be enforced with positive thoughts about all of your beautiful qualities and grateful memories of past experiences.

Wearing a smile invites love into your life. It will instantly make you feel happier and more in tune with connecting among social peers.

4. Keep Good Posture

Much like smiling, maintaining good posture in a social setting plays an important role. Body language is as important as the words that are being said in the conversation. It also establishes your control over the social situation. Whether you're sitting or standing in front of your audience, you need to work hard to improve your posture.

A chjuykchesr hadest out, back straight either sitting or standing and a head held high posture communicates confidence, relaxation, makes you appear more prominent and will immediately put those around you at ease. It also gives you the added benefit of aligning your body so you can breathe which will result in you speaking efficiently. It takes some monitoring and demands a lot of practice to get into the habit of good posture if you're a bit of a sloucher, but the result is well worth it.

5.Maintain Eye Contact

Eye contact shows the other party that you're legitimately interested in what

they're saying. Failing to make eye contact suggests to some that you're shy; to others, it indicates rudeness or boredom. This becomes especially important for a job interview.

By not maintaining eye contact, you may give the impression that you're trying to hide something. This translates directly to lack of confidence.

It's almost impossible to stare into both a person's eyes simultaneously so pick one and stick with it. Keep eye contact short but frequent, looking away when you feel the need but always returning and appearing interested.

If you feel anxious, take short breaks to look away and then refocus on the person's eye. Remember, if you're genuinely interested in what the person has to say, there's no reason to feel nervous. Your sincerity will show through because you're paying attention.

6. Be Agreeable

When confrontation arises in a conversation, sometimes it can feel awkward to disagree. After all, you're entitled to having your own opinion, but you may not want to offend the other party.

An excellent way to disagree without creating tension is to use a third party to be disagreeable. It makes you appear to be on the person's side but with acknowledgment to the difference in opinion.

For example, let's say the person says "I think this band is terrible!"

You could say - "I heard on Yahoo news that they just sold out Madison Square Garden." If you don't want to interject your opinion harshly, this is a flexible way to engage in differing views.

Gesticulate.

Gesticulations involve using your hands and arms to give punctuation or enhance your verbal statements. It is another valuable body language strategy. When you make use of body language very often in your conversation and punctuation, you'll be viewed as more confident and more authoritative than those who do not.

Try to use your hand gestures for your most impactful words, and try to keep your movements reserved and under strict control.

Speak more slowly

When we're nervous, you tend to speak faster to hide your nervousness. You may be a fast talker naturally. But talking soon, either conscious or subconsciously shows a lack of confidence or a lack of authority. Moreover, if you are sputtering, you're more likely to make mistakes in your pronunciation, and you would not have much time to think through your words. You should try to place more focus on speaking more slowly in your conversation, allow your words to settle and give your sentences a weightier rhythm. When you talk slowly, your audience will have more time to digest the information you're passing, and you'll be less likely to make any compelling errors that will compromise your speaking integrity.

Take advantage of pauses

Using pauses in a conversation is an action that can help you speak slower, but it has a different effect. Learn to use breaks creatively to give more impact to your speaking. Let's say you have an opening for a public presentation, and after making a few sentences, you throw in a significant point and then go on a few seconds pause. This technique will make your last sentence have more weight, and your audience will absorb it more. You're also given a chance to collect your thoughts and prepare for the next section. This will add to the previous amount of confidence and authority you project.

Chapter Five

Surviving Real Life Situations

The lectures and skill sets acquired in this guide are universal in practice. They are tailored to be used in every scenarios and situation we find ourselves. People with social anxieties are humans living everyday human lives, plunged into everyday human settings and looking for ways to live and survive through it all. That is where this book and guide comes into play. However, some situations require just a bit of extra tact. That's why I've implemented this section on how to survive specific daily or occasional scenarios that can cause social anxiety to flare up. So, follow along and think of the guidelines below as just that – guidelines. These are not hard and fast rules for you to abide by. The idea of managing social anxiety is based on finding your comfort zone. Use the tips below as touchstones for you to fall back on when you feel discomfort arise.

Whether you are working, schooling or whatever you do that involves interaction with other people, and this book is tailored to handle it.

At The Workplace

In a work situation, you are being evaluated based on your performance, which is what a socially anxious person dreads the most. And, it's unfortunately true, people actually may start to react to you differently if you are withdrawn at work depending on the political climate.

The effect may cause you to become more withdrawn and sometimes even angry. So, how do you deal with the work environment?

Developing a routine with standard social situations at work is a good strategy. Have a game plan for the day, and things will immediately feel more in your control.

Business Meetings

If you feel uncomfortable in meetings, try arriving 10 to 15 minutes early so that you can meet people as they come.

This is the opposite of what most shy people do -- they tend to show up late so that they don't have to engage in small talk with others in the meeting. This intervention connotes the unintended ore effect of making you feel more isolated.

Social Functions

Depending on your place of employment, there may be an endless array of social functions that you are expected to attend; the company picnic, the annual Christmas party, retirement gatherings, and business lunches, for example.

Preparation will be your best ally in these situations. Make sure that you have something to talk about. Read the newspaper, visit an online news source, or read current magazines.

Above all, avoid using alcohol to overcome your inhibitions. Often just the passage of time will have the same effect on reducing inhibitions as consuming alcohol. Drinking will only lead to feelings of regret the next day over what you think you may have said or how you may feel you acted.

Daily Interactions

The only way to ultimately become more comfortable with coworkers is to strive to expand your comfort zones continually.

Engage in small talk with people that you see throughout the day -- in the lunchroom, in the elevator, and even as cliché as it may sound -- at the water cooler.

Greet people with general comments or compliments and start brief conversations. Gradually this act will become more comfortable and more relaxed. You'll also feel a great sense of accomplishment after taking such a leap to overcome your social phobia. It may seem challenging at first, but you know what they say? No pain, no gain. This exercise will build your social muscles and make way for more comfortable future conversations.

Job Interviews

Going on a job interview can shake the nerves of even the calmest individual, let alone that of a social anxiety sufferer. So, how do you get through it? Well, there are some handy coping mechanisms you can use when the anxiety becomes overwhelming.

Start on the right foot. Avoid caffeine, get enough sleep, and exercise regularly. By following these three simple rules, you will significantly reduce job interview anxiety. You'll walk in the door more relaxed and in a better state of mind to answer questions calmly.

Visualize your success. This means more than just positive thinking. You're getting your brain ready to behave in the way that you desire. This technique is used by elite athletes before competitions to improve performance, and it can work for you too. Focus on your strong suits and advantages and keep your mind around that, don't think much about your weaknesses.

Think about how you will project your voice, your posture, your enthusiasm for the job opportunity. This way you will translate well when you sit down and go through the motions with the interviewer.

Reduce your stress. Keep your clothing as comfortable as possible. Make sure you know how to get to the interview location without getting lost. Give yourself plenty of time to find it or do a trial run a day or two before. Show up with plenty of time to spare to avoid being late. These are all things you can do to ensure when you show up; there are no distractions to stress you out. You can solely concentrate on the task at hand; landing that fantastic job.

Do Your Research is the most crucial part of preparing for the interview. Know the answers to common interview questions like:

"What are your greatest strengths?" "What is your greatest weakness?" "Why do you want this job?"

"Why do you think you're the best candidate for this job?" "What kind of experience do you have related to this position?" "What was your single biggest work-related accomplishment?" "Where do you see yourself in 5 years professionally?"

"Who are your biggest influences?"

"What was the last problem you solved at work?" "Do you enjoy working in teams?"

"When can you start?"

"What do you know about this company?"

These are general questions that you should know the answers to before you go into the interview. Invest the time to think of impressive, refreshingly honest answers that will wow your interviewer. Rehearsing answering questions like this will put your brain into interview mode, and the outcome will be well worth the time you put in.

The First Date

You tried to get her number – you were nervous. You spoke on the phone – you were shy -Now you've arranged to meet up. You're even more nervous. Calm down, first date anxiety is normal. Here are some tips to make it more enjoyable.

There is some good news. The common link between people of all levels of anxiety is that as time increases stress almost always decreases, so, the longer your date goes on, the more comfortable you're going to get.

Take deep breaths. The other person is just as nervous as you are. They are also eager and anxious of pleasing, not fumbling, and of being seen in a good light. You are not alone. So, just take a deep breathe and relax.

Count to three, fill your lungs, then breathe out. Don't forget that last part. It's the long, deep exhalation that makes the difference. Consciously taking control of your breathing helps override your autonomic nervous system, leading to a decrease in the butterflies in your stomach. You want to engage in this exercise before the date. You don't want to look like dinner is making you hyperventilate.

What's the worst that could happen?

Be honest with yourself. What's the worst that could happen?

Focusing on the worst possible scenario helps you deal with this irrational component. On a first date, what's the worst that could happen? Maybe she won't like you; perhaps you'll embarrass yourself. Whatever it is, you'll be laughing about it in a couple of weeks and it will just be a humorous story to reflect upon.

That brings me to another tip. It's crucial to have a sense of humor about yourself, particularly on a date. Don't take yourself so seriously. Life is too short to worry over every little detail. Try to have fun with it and be in the moment.

This isn't your last first date.

You probably don't want to be reminded of the expression 'plenty more fish in the sea,' but it's true. While you may think you've found your ideal match, the truth is someone you like even more might come along next week.

Take what you learn on your date and try again. Think of it as on the job training. There will be more first dates, and the more you practice, the better you'll get.

Eventually, you'll level up. It's called the 'dating game' for a reason. Play it, and you will improve.

Party Time

I thought parties were supposed to be fun? So, why is it that you get a big ole' pit of anxiety in your belly to moment you find out there's a gathering to attend?

Parties mean socializing and that confrontation can bring about social anxiety before there's even a person to talk to. Try these strategies.

Start thinking early about how you will spend your time relaxing before the party. If possible, make sure that you have at least a few hours of downtime to prepare. Try pampering yourself with whatever pleases you. Some ideas might be working out, reading a good book or engaging in a favorite hobby.

Has an outfit planned well ahead of time? Know the dress code.

Choose clothing that both looks good on you and that is comfortable. You want to increase your confidence by wearing clothes that are flattering and make you feel good.

Is a gift required? Pick it up with lots of time to spare. The last thing you need is stressing out before the party because you don't have a gift of just found out you don't have wrapping paper. Cut down on your anxiety by having the present in order long before the affair.

Arrive earlier than later. Although you don't want to get to a party inappropriately early, it's better to lean on the first side. Walking into space is less uncomfortable and socially awkward than walking into a large crowded room of people. It's a simple way to ease your way into the social setting as the crowd grows after you've already arrived.

You are approaching people. If you find yourself at a party where you don't know anyone (hats off to you for going!) the first challenge will be to finding someone to talk to. Look for a friendly face in the crowd. Maybe there is someone else who also appears to be alone.

Make a general comment about your surroundings such as:

"This place is pretty cool," or

"How do you know so and so."

If the person does not reciprocate or start up a conversation, try again with someone else.

It's best to meet people at a party on a one on one basis rather than trying to approach a small group. Look for stragglers. If you see someone break apart from a group, try contacting that person one-on-one. Be aware of your body language in addition to what you say.

Try not to cross your arms and make sure to have a smile on your face. Ideally, that person will introduce you to the rest of the group, and you'll begin making more connections at the party.

The conversation should start light and get more specific when prompted. If you're speaking with people you don't know, try to gauge their interests. Talking about current events, favorite movies, music, sports, restaurants or commonalities (if you both have kids or a similar career) are high introductory points.

Have an exit strategy. Have a plan ahead of time as to how and when you will leave the party. If you're having fun, you can and should try to stay longer, but knowing you have a time set to go will decrease the anxiety of the situation and give you a hard stop where you can step away and relax. Don't forget to congratulate yourself for making an effort to face your social anxiety head-on.

Family Gatherings

There's usually a lot of people; there are the poking and prodding in your life, the staring, and everything else that can make you nervous. I'd usually do anything to avoid conversation. I would suddenly become more productive - cleaning and washing dishes. But you can still never 100% prevent the interaction. So, what's the best way to get through it?

If the gathering is at your house, try distracting yourself with chores while the company is over – but stay in the same room as the guests.

For example, if there are dishes in the sink, you can wash them. If there are garbage bags to be replaced, you can do that. It will allow you to have something to do with your nervous energy, yet still, keep you engaged with the company.

You may have to go slowly with family members that have specific quirks or are hard to deal with. You won't be able to change them in the length of one party so helping yourself to remain calm and balanced is the best step you can take for everyone involved.

We all have that one family member that knows how to push our buttons. If you feel stressed at the thought consider ways to distance yourself and get involved in other family conversations or activities.

Have an escape plan but use it only when you need it. You don't want to spend the better half of Thanksgiving hiding in the bathroom from your crazy Aunt Helen.

A huge part of preparing for family gatherings is making sure your body and mind are as relaxed as possible. You should engage in as many relaxation techniques as possible. I'll be showing you how to do this in the next section.

Above all, try to remember that this kooky clan is, in fact, your family. Deep down they love you very much, and as much as they may stress you out socially, it's coming from the right place. Rise above the situation by recognizing them for what they are – the lovable contributors of your unique blend of DNA. Practice some patience and them day will be more bearable than you initially anticipated.

Chapter Six

Overcoming the Physical Symptoms of Social Anxiety

The initial phases of social anxiety can come on with similar symptoms of a panic attack. Your adrenaline may start to race through your veins. Your voice may

become shaky and shrill with nerves. It's possible you begin to sweat excessively or blush.

Other symptoms include dizziness, difficulty swallowing or speaking and even stuttering.

Here are some ways to quiet your nerves and condition your mind to remain calm when social anxiety creates these kinds of physical symptoms. They work very well but do require some practice on your part.

Also, these relaxation exercises should be performed before engaging in social settings to prepare your body or regularly, daily to condition your body and mind into a more relaxed state of being.

Breathing

A lot of changes happen in your body when you feel anxious. One of the first is that your breathing changes and this throws off the carbon dioxide and oxygen in your body which gives way for other physical symptoms. You can relieve the tension by practicing the technique below.

Sit comfortably with your back straightened up, and your shoulders relaxed. Put one hand on your chest and the other on your stomach.

Take a moment to close your eyes and focus only on your breathing. Inhale slowly through your nose for about four minutes.

Feel your diaphragm move up into your ribcage and extend your belly outward as you inhale. Slowly push out you're breathing as you exhale through your mouth.

Feel the stress being breathed out of your body. It is no longer a part of you. Each breath should take 6 seconds to complete.

Spend 3 seconds slowly inhaling through your nose and the other 3 seconds slowly exhaling through your mouth. Take 5-10 breaths like this, and you'll instantly feel more relaxed.

Meditation

Take a few minutes to think about all the things you are grateful for. It could be as simple as feeling grateful for the food in your fridge or the way your puppy dog loves you.

Take the time to appreciate all the gifts you have in life and how lucky you are to have them.

When you show thanks for good in your life, more good will attract itself to you. I spend 5 minutes every morning meditating on gratitude while I take a shower. It's amazing how it always starts me off in such an excellent mood for the day.

Exercise

Although Cardio Exercise like running or bike riding is more effective for relieving anxiety, weight lifting works well too. Just getting to the gym in general.

And burning off some steam is a beautiful way to feel better. Exercise doesn't just provide a physical release.

You're also providing a mental release as well. By exercising, you counterbalance your negative thoughts with a positive feeling that you are taking steps towards improving your health. In effect, you cast aside worry and calm your mind with the natural high of working out.

Do Charity Work

When you help others, you take the focus off yourself. Taking the focus off yourself is a big part of overcoming anxiety. You internalize less and merely live in the moment, taking pleasure in the world around you. Feel good about yourself for doing a positive thing for others. When you volunteer, or do charity works, you fill up your time and you are more active. Another benefit is that you feel good helping other people, it comes in handy in the future when you start to internalize and contemplate about life.

With charity work, you are not just helping others. You are helping yourself too.

Write Out Your Thoughts

If you feel anxious or upset, write down your thoughts in a letter or diary.

Sometimes, getting it all out on paper can feel like you're getting out of your system. Don't meditate on your negative thoughts. Merely spill them out in front of you. Feel the words leaving your mind, making room for a more peaceful state of consciousness.

Stretch

Every night before bed, take 5 minutes to stretch. Even if it's just touching your toes, every bit helps. When you stretch, you relieve tension in your back and muscles. You'll feel calmer and more relaxed instantly.

It is also a great way to prepare for a fantastic night's sleep. If you prefer not to stretch right before bed, you can do so before going to the gym. It helps circulation and prevents injury as well. This anxiety reliever takes just minutes, and it does wonders.

As a side benefit, you'll feel so much better physically. Since I started stretching, I've noticed significantly fewer muscle cramps and soreness after a workout. I can honestly say this technique has made me feel younger and more vibrant.

Repeat a Mantra

As the Law of Attraction States, thoughts are things. So when you think negatively, negative things will come into your life. Conversely, when you think positively, positive things will come into your life. Having a Mantra is a great way to control your thought pattern and relieve anxiety.

When you're feeling anxious, have a mantra, or short prayer memorized that you can repeat at the moment. Every person's mantra will be different and tailored to their anxiety, but my mantra is: "I am a kind, loving person.

I strive every day to be the best I can be, and all good things flow to me from the universe. Any worry or stress I have now will not make a difference in the long term.

Of my life. My life is good and will continue to be good. I am blessed for all that I have. The only opinion that matters in life is the opinion of myself. I love myself." You can make your mantra whatever you choose. Make it something that speaks to your mentality and comforts your soul. Repeat your mantra in times of doubt and confusion. Hold firm that it is the truth. Your mantra will be your relaxing touchstone.

Avoid Caffeine

While this may sound like a bit of a tough one, it is very much doable. I used to be a bit of a caffeine addict. And guess what? It was right around the same time my anxiety was at its worst. Sound like a coincidence?

Not really. It's easy to think that caffeine heightens your mood. After all, it's a stimulant. But the crash that you get from a strong caffeine high is enough to bring on extreme anxiety and depression.

So do yourself a favor and start weaning yourself off the caffeine train. I now begin every morning with Green Tea, and I eat a Granny Smith apple with my breakfast.

Granny Smiths have been proven to wake you up just as much as a cup of coffee in the morning.

Drink Green Tea

L-theanine is an amino acid found in tea plants. It also promotes relaxation and modifies the stimulating effects of the caffeine present in green tea. What does that mean exactly?

Well, L-theanine is a caffeine antagonist, meaning that it offsets the "hyper" effect of caffeine. That is why many people will have a "soothing" cup of tea and not a soothing cup of coffee. Green tea contains more theanine than the other drinks.

Try drinking Green Tea in the morning for a more gradual and calming wake-up boost.

Listen to Music

Sit back and relax to your favorite tunes. I love listening to classic rock. If you're feeling nostalgic, put on something that will transport you to another place in time. Escape and think of nothing but the music. Try to play songs with a positive or uplifting message. It's up to you. Just enjoy and have fun.

Being able to relax in a social setting, means having the ability to put your body and mind into a more peaceful state. To accomplish this, you'll want to practice the exercises above and being to understand the relaxation triggers that put you at ease. Once you know that, you can call upon these triggers as you need them.

10 Ways to Improve Your Self Esteem

Here, I'm going to show you 10 LIFECHANGING tips for improving self-esteem. And let me say before we delve into it that EVERYONE can benefit from these tips. Also – I want to point out that I just said 10 LIFE CHANGING tips.

That's because self-esteem is a characteristic that genuinely SHAPES your life. Self-esteem builds confidence and allows you to BE who you are. It will enable you to be true to yourself – in every way.

So with that said, here are ten great principles to improve your self-esteem and boost your feelings of self-worth through continued practice.

Quick Disclaimer Here - Be aware that just knowing the info I'm about to reveal won't be enough to raise self-esteem. You have to go through the motions and practice what I'm about to preach. By taking action on these tips, you'll feel a LOT better in time.

So here we go with tip #1

1. Stop Comparing Yourself.

I'm sure at one time or another, you've looked at your neighbor, friend, family member or co-worker with envious eyes. You've been enamored with someone else's big salary, picturesque family life, perfect looks, ripped 6-pack – whatever. Everyone on occasion falls victim to feeling inadequate as a result of someone else's accomplishments.

I'm going to tell you right now if you want to improve your self-esteem, the very first thing you need to do is throw this habit out the window.

Stop comparing yourself to other people. Be your person and love the skin you're in.

When you compare yourself with others, only two possible outcomes can arise.

The first outcome is, you compare yourself with someone less fortunate than you. Now, this can bring about feelings of gratitude where you learn to appreciate what you have, and THIS scenario can have the effect of boosting your self-esteem – which is good.

The problem is, when you become accustomed to this comparing mentality, you'll start more often than not comparing yourself to people who have qualities that you don't possess.

More money, less weight, fancier cars, attractive counterparts, career, children – there are endless factors that makeup who we are. And when you start comparing yourself with other people, you'll tend to focus on the factors that you envy rather than the strengths and fortune that you already possess.

2. Keep Your Thoughts Positive.

We all have a constant monologue running through our brain. It's just impossible to turn off that inner voice. If you're constantly thinking negative thoughts that reinforce feelings of low self-esteem, the result will be just that.

It's so important to stay aware of your thinking and not to fall into the habit of self-deprecation or talking down to yourself.

Look for your strengths in everyday life and make it a practice to continually pat yourself on the back for all your amazing qualities.

You've got to create a habit here. And that's the habit of self-appreciation. You can begin this new way of thinking every morning in the shower. The shower is a great place to spend (even just 5 minutes) meditating on how good you are. Congratulate yourself on every victory or success – no matter how small. Every little self-compliment will add up to greater feelings of self-worth.

Try using affirmations too.

It forces you to engage in the exercise through a dependable mantra. Using affirmations doesn't have to be complicated.

You don't have to repeat a wild chant or a longwinded prayer to use this strategy.

An affirmation is merely a way of asserting your confidence with a statement. When you repeat an affirmation, you're essentially confirming a belief in yourself out loud. It can feel silly the first time you do it, but it is a healthy way to exercise your self-esteem.

Once again, the morning shower is a great way to work this practice into your life without taking up a lot of time.

One of the easiest ways to use affirmations is to make short lists of positive factors in your life.

For example. You could say: I am an excellent listener, a talented artist, a hard worker, a kind person, well read, fabulous in the kitchen, have beautiful teeth whatever.

Just list out the qualities that make you feel good about yourself. Feel proud as you reflect on your good fortune. Feel good to be you.

3. Accept All Compliments with Thank You.

You may find that a lot of times, you'll receive a

compliment and respond with "Oh, it was nothing" or "It's no big deal" etc. I want you to know that this is a crucial way to sabotage self-esteem.

When you mostly refuse a compliment, you're telling yourself that you're not worth the praise. You devalue yourself.

I know this may sound overdramatic. You're not thinking at the time that the compliment is given "Oh I'm not worthy of this praise" but in fact,

the action turning down the compliment by brushing it off sends a message to your subconscious brain which in turn lessens your confidence and feelings of self-worth.

You're reinforcing the bad by not embracing the good.

Instead, accept every compliment with Thank You. It's a simple answer that will allow you to feel good about yourself and satisfy the person giving the praise. So remember, you can't lose by saying Thank you.

4. Find Positive Input

It's so important to engage in activities that make you feel good. Read books that inspire you, watch movies that make you laugh.

One thing I like to do is watch some motivational or inspirational clip on Youtube every week. And it's something that puts my mind in a hopeful, positive light.

Another way to find positive input is to create a new challenge for yourself. It could be something like learning a new language, mastering a skill or just working towards self-improvement in some area of your life.

5. Associate with Supportive People

Nothing lowers self-esteem faster than associating with

people who make you feel bad about yourself. Unfortunately, this is a common scenario for people with low self-esteem. They tend to group with people who they seek approval from.

It's a scenario that sabotages self-worth because they'll always be worried about what members of the group think of them.

Break this habit by finding people who love you from the getgo. Hang out with people who accept you unconditionally and respect who you are.

By the way, this won't happen until YOU respect who you are. So work towards that goal first.

6. Make a List of Past Successes

A great way to exercise self-esteem is to celebrate all of your past successes. Take the time to write down all your accomplishments (no matter how small) and bask in the light of your achievements. Seeing your progress on paper can make even the most modest victory more gratifying.

7. List Your Positive Qualities

Much like the last tip, seeing how awesome you are on paper is excellent. However, this tip has the bonus of showing you what kind of person you are. By knowing your strengths, you'll be able to focus on actions that give you positive results in life.

As illustrated by the picture here, this strategy works well in both personal life AND business.

8. Do Good For Others

Day to day life presents us with opportunities to do good deeds for others. It could be someone who needs help opening a door, someone who needs help finding exact change for that vending machine in your office's break room. Whatever the situation, no matter how big or small, choose to help when you can.

You'll feel better for it.

9. Find Your Passion

We all feel better when we're productive. After finding your strengths through some of the exercises listed above, you'll know where your skills pack the biggest punch.

Find your passion in business, volunteer work, school or study and fortify your feelings of self-worth. Everyone has a talent. Everyone has skill. Know yourself and follow your heart.

10. Be true to yourself.

Staying true to your character in any situation is what defines your integrity. Be moral. Be kind and strive to do the right thing in any case. When you have a strong moral compass, you'll always be comfortable in your skin.

Chapter Seven

Getting Out There

The only way to get over social anxiety is to get out there and start exposing yourself to uncomfortable situations. The idea of exposing yourself to stress triggers to overcome them is based on a practice known as cognitive behavioral therapy.

In this therapy method, you face your fears head on, and the result is your anxiety decreases with each exposure. The stress becomes less the more you engage in social situations because you'll be exercising the control techniques outlined in this system.

See, you can learn every social anxiety tip and trick in the world, but none of it will do you any good unless you use the tools in the real world and field test this stuff.

Here we'll be discussing some gradual and safe ways to begin engaging in social situations without diving right into the deep end of the pool.

You might be thinking that immediate immersion in a social crowd sounds terrifying but when you take these baby steps, you'll slowly acclimate yourself to the idea of getting out there.

Start Smiling More

Smiling is a tip I provide when talking about building conversational confidence and self-esteem. It's also an engaging way to connect with others.

The best way to begin is to catch the eye of someone walking in passing. It could be at an office building, at school or even just a random person on the street.

Give the other person a warm smile. Nothing creepy. Just a pleasant "Good Day to you" kind of smile. You'll be surprised to see how many people smile right back.

Try not to glare after smiling. Just give people a sweet, pleasant smile and look away after giving them enough time to reciprocate. If they don't smile back don't feel bad — you've already benefitted from this exercise by just putting yourself out there.

This exercise builds human guts. It strengthens your mental muscles and puts you into a more outgoing mindset.

You can even turn this into a game for encouragement. See how many people you can get to smile at you with this technique. 1? 5? 10? Try to outdo yourself as time and experience progress.

Do You Know What Time It Is?

Using common questions to strangers or people around you is an easy way to open the door to a pleasant conversation. Remember, questions are your friend. They allow you to steer the direction of conversation so use this to your advantage.

Questions like, *"Do you know what time it is?"* *"Beautiful weather, isn't it?" Have you seen (insert movie title)?"* are simple, gentle ways to invite people into connecting with you kindly. I've listed below some easy one-liners to get a conversation rolling if you ever hit an awkward pause or have trouble getting started.

Hi, I'm (insert name). It's nice to meet you. Hello, how are you?

Where are you from?

Hi, what have you been up to since I last saw you? Good to finally meet you, how have you been?

What line of work are you in? Do you have kids?

Where did you grow up?

Hey, crazy weather we've been having.

Hi, good to see you again. Hey, I like your jacket/bag/shoes, etc.

Who do you admire as a leader?

What is the best compliment you have received? What movie can you watch over and over again?

If you were to write a novel what would it be about? What is your favorite dessert?

If you had your TV network what would you put on it? If you could be any age what age would you choose?

What is the stupidest thing that one of your friends has done?

If we had an extra room in our home what do you think we should use it for? What religion other than our own do you think is fascinating?

What makes a house a home?

Where do you what to live when you are on your own? What is something you are good at?

Who was the last person who had a crush on you?

If you needed someone to act as a character reference

who will you pick? Who do you turn to for advice?

What goals do you have for your education?

If we have guests in from out of town what do you think we should show them?

Online Forums

If the thought of approaching someone in public is too much to bear, you can take baby steps with online forums. Find a topic you're interested and type in that topic name followed by forums in Google's search.

There are forums everywhere based on all sorts of interests.

Start up an online chat or thread in the forum and start building rapport with other forum members. The act will give you confidence in your ability to steer a conversation. You can practice some of the methods discussed here to control

And flow the conversations with other members. It will ultimately empower you to take the plunge in real life with people all around you.

Online Dating

Dating and social anxiety are a tough combination to overcome. And, the act of hitting on a random stranger without social confidence is a surefire way to bring on feelings of doubt and low self-esteem.

An excellent way to initiate meeting people is going the online route. In the beginning, it's much less confrontational, and you have the opportunity to get to know someone a bit before the overwhelming face to face gets together.

Having the opportunity to build a certain level of rapport before meeting people, or just socializing in this medium rich with forum buddies is ideal.

Online dating softens the blow of social anxiety by allowing you time to prepare for your final meeting. You can practice the exercises in this guide with the specific person in mind, and they'll be much more effective because, at this point, you're already familiar with the person's interests, desires and sense of humor.

Just Do It

Whatever approach you take the most important thing is getting out there and subjecting yourself to social dynamics. It's a good idea to have a rock-solid philosophy on how to handle rejection and disappointment so that if and when they arise, you won't be derailed entirely from your efforts to be more social.

Try to understand that not everyone will click with your personality and that's okay. You need to be willing to fail a bit before you find success in your social circle. It's the only way.

Benjamin Franklin had a saying that the only way to speed your way to success is to increase your rate of failure. You have to find out what doesn't work so you can settle into your own social pace.

Once you do find your way, you'll realize how much more comfortable you are in your skin, embracing all your quirks, flaws and imperfections. After all, those are the things that make you, you!

And, you're great. So love yourself and love being in the moment. Get out there, take risks and find social success.Try to understand that not everyone will click with your personality and that's okay. You need to be willing to fail a bit before you find success in your social circle. Really, it's the only way.

Benjamin Franklin had a saying that the only way to speed your way to success is to increase your rate of failure. You have to find out what doesn't work so you can settle in to your own social pace.

Once you do find your way, you'll realize how much more comfortable you are in your own skin, embracing all your quirks, flaws and imperfections. After all, those are the things that make you, *you*!

And, you're great. So love yourself and love being in the moment. Get out there, take risks and find social success.

Chapter Eight

Depression

Depression is a widespread and severe medical or mental illness that affects how you feel, think and act, negatively. Depression causes intense sadness, and a depressed person loses interest in a lot of activities that were once enjoyed. A depressed person usually goes through a lot of emotional and physical problems and have trouble functioning at home or work. Depression is a sad state that is synonymous with people suffering from social anxiety. It is a state of mind that fills you with self-loathing, self-destruction as you beat yourself up and slump more in-depth into the caves of depression.

Symptoms of depression include;

There are a lot of signs that show you are suffering from depression. Depression is not something that hides; it is not something that you go to a professional or under the x-ray to notice. You feel it, you see it. The following are its symptoms.

-Feeling sad or low: You tend to feel beaten, defeated and broken. Depression comes with a deep feeling of sadness, self-loathing, self-hate and self condescension.

-Loss of interest in activities previously found pleasurable: When you are depressed, you.begin to lose interest in activities and hobbies you used to have immense importance in.

-Appetite change leading to weight loss or gain

-Sleep issues - too much or too little

-Energy loss/ Excessive fatigue

-Increase in purposeless physical activity (e.g., hand-wringing or pacing) or slowed movements and speech (actions observable by others)

-Feeling worthless or guilty

-Difficulty thinking, concentrating or making decisions

-Thoughts of death or suicide

The symptoms must be present for up to two weeks before a diagnosis of depression is made. Depression symptoms can exert their toll on you and make it extremely difficult for you to attend to normal daily activities and hurts employment or Schooling, and other areas of functioning.

Types of depression

To some people, depression is just limited to clinical depression and the one every other person suffers from. But depression can be classified into five different types.

Major depression

Major depression is the type most people call clinical depression or just 'depression.' It is characterized by low mood and loss of interest and pleasure in regular activities. The symptoms are experienced in most days and last for a minimum of two weeks. It interferes with every area of the individual's life. Depression can be described as mild, moderate or severe.

Severe depression can also be called melancholia. When a person has melancholy, it means that many of the physical symptoms of depression are present. The person begins to move more slowly and sinks into a low mood where they lose complete pleasure and interest in everything or almost everything.

Psychotic depression is also another type of severe depression. Most times people with depressive disorder can lose contact with reality and experience psychosis. Then they may begin to have hallucinations, or delusions, such as believing they are wrong or evil and are being followed or watched. They may also experience paranoia blaming everyone around them for being the cause of their illness or the adverse events happening around them.

Antenatal and postnatal depression

Women are at an increased risk of depression, prenatally and potentially. There are complex reasons why they enter depression. Depression is different from the 'baby blues' or general stress that occur in most women following childbirth. Depression is usually longer lasting and affects both the mother and her relationship with her baby, the child's development, the mother's relationship with her partner and other members of the family.

Bipolar disorder

Bipolar disorder was previously known as 'manic depression' because the person goes through periods of depression and periods of mania with some periods of good mood in between.

Mania can make a person feel great all of a sudden, have lots of energy, racing thoughts and little need for sleep. It presents as the opposite of depression. Sometimes the person loses touch with reality and drifts towards psychosis having hallucinations and delusions.

Depression and social anxiety

Although social anxiety can be caused by its reasons, depression has a very close relationship with it. People usually wonder if depression is caused by social anxiety or if the reverse is the case and it is depression that leads to social anxiety.

Social anxiety disorder (social phobia) is intense anxiety or fear of being judged or rejected in a social setting. Those with a social anxiety disorder may be worried about acting visibly anxious or being perceived as stupid and awkward by others. Because of this, they often avoid social or performance situations and experience significant anxiety and distress in unavoidable circumstances.

Feeling anxious and worried about being with people can escalate into feeling down generally especially when you start isolating yourself and stop participating in activities. However, there are some symptoms of depression that can also make one fear of being around people for specific reasons.

If you have social anxiety, the chances are that you'd develop depression as the years go by.

The usual process is that it begins when you become socially fearful, then start staying away from social situations, and consequently develop a depressed mood due to social isolation.

Some symptoms of depression are similar to that of social anxiety and act as a stepping stone from one of the disorders to the other. Some of these symptoms are pointed out below.

I am getting anxious when in an embarrassing situation with a specific person.

Anxiety when having to speak in the presence of a specific other people

Inability to feel happy which is detected by not being cheerful or not being able to laugh easily.

Feelings of worthlessness or guilt

Irritability

Unstable mood and depressed mood reduced interest or pleasure in activities previously enjoyed, loss of sexual desire unintentional weight loss (without dieting) or low appetite insomnia (difficulty sleeping) or hypersomnia (excessive sleeping) psychomotor agitation, for example, restlessness, pacing up and down delayed psychomotor skills, for example, slowed movement and speech fatigue or loss of energy impaired ability to think, concentrate, or make decisions recurrent thoughts of death or suicide, or attempt at suicide

Causes of depression

Depression cannot be pinpointed to an exact reason but are a lot of things that have been associated with its emergence in an individual. It usually originates from a combination of recent events that have been around for a long while.

The causes range from issues involving personal factors and may sometimes be due to the increased genetic risk.

Family history – Depression runs in some families putting some people at an increased genetic risk. It does not mean that when you have a parent or close relative with Depression you'll automatically experience it. Life circumstances still have a role to play. Depression can also develop in individuals who have conflicts or disputes with family members or friends. A person who has experienced the loss or death of a loved one can be plunged into grief which may cause depression.

Personality – People who tend to worry a lot, have low self-esteem, are perfectionists, are sensitive to personal criticism, or harmful is more as the risk of depression because of their personality. People who have experienced physical, sexual or emotional abuse are vulnerable to depression too.

Serious medical illness – Those who have the severe disease are prone to having depression. When you're dealing with long-term management and chronic pain which causes worry or stress, you might end up being depressed.

Drug and alcohol use – Drug and alcohol use can lead to depression. Even if drugs or alcohol temporarily make you feel better, they ultimately will aggravate depression.

Changes in the brain

Some people fall into depression because of genetic vulnerability and severe life dressers. Some times the substances you take (some medications, drugs, and alcohol) and certain medical conditions can affect the way your brain regulates your mood, leading to a depressed feeling.

Depression and Human Relationship

Depression can make it tedious to maintain supportive and fulfilling relationships. When you're in a continuous lousy mood, everything seems bleak, including your links. When you're having problems with your relationship, you are more likely to feel sad and anxious. It means that there is a connection between your emotion and relationships.

If you want to know how your mood is creating problems in your relationship, then you should begin to take note of what others say to you. Similarly, when you tend to see only the dark side of a situation, it can affect your relationship with those who love you.

Even if you're not the depressed one, but you have a partner suffering from depression, their symptoms may overwhelm them and make them lose the energy to communicate. It might be upsetting and draining leading you to exhaustion as you need to support your partner and also keep up with other affairs.

In turn, the depressed person may begin to feel like a burden as if they were getting in the way and worsening the lives of those around them. They may resent the effect of their depression on their relationship but are incapable of doing anything about it. The whole scenario might even make them feel guilty thereby lowering their self-esteem

How To Help Depressed People

If you happen to be related or in a relationship with a depressed person, there are some things you could do to assist them. This tips also apply to self-usage. You can use these tips to defeat depression when it comes. And soon, sit it out entirely and get back control of your life.

Open communication.

Mental health issues place pressure on relationships, and this can be eased by talking openly and honestly about the difficulties each partner is facing. Open communication with friends, with lovers and family, do not succumb to the voice or idea of shutting everyone out. It is time you need people most, to talk to people, to play and be around people more. You need their energies to fuel you and shake you off the shackles of depression.

Externalizing

You should be able to detach the condition from the person. Treat it and refer to it as a different entity from the individual. The goal is to help the depressed person see it as separate rather than part of their personality.

Breaking down the details

You should also identify the exact nature of the depression, know the triggers and understand it's severity. Most people who feel like depression affects them all the time realize that there are times when it's not an issue and times when it is severe. When you find out what leads to stress or depression, you can know how to help.

Making a timeline together

Look at the positive and negative events throughout the relationship and try to locate when the depression first intruded itself into the relationship. It could've been cashed by a loss of something or someone. With the timeline, each partner can understand how the other is feeling.

Tips For Living With Depression

If you are dealing with depression, always remember that you are not alone. There are millions of people around the world who also live with depression.

Dealing with depression is a lifelong journey of overcoming pain, accepting change and challenging your mind. You can also train your body to engage in something outside of yourself.

When you're going through depression, even the slightest thing feels more challenging. Socializing with friends, going to work, doing extra activities or also just getting out of bed feels like a struggle. But you can do some things to cope with your symptoms and quality of life. Here are some tips that can help you live with depression.

Try Not to Beat Up on Yourself

Depressed people sometimes blame themselves for having it. Then they beat up on themselves for making the mistakes they believe led to the depression. This act makes it worse. It might make them act in ways they deem unacceptable, and they may criticize themselves too. If you're depressed, you should try not to blame yourself for it so you can feel better.

Build a Support Network

To help yourself with depression, an important thing to do after medication and therapy is developing strong social support. It might involve strengthening ties with friends and family. When you have supportive people who you can count will go a long way in improving your depression.

Apart from family, you can join a depression support group. It may be within the community or online.

Reduce your stress

Your body produces a hormone called cortisol when you're stressed. Cortisol is good only in the short term because it helps you prepare to cope with the stress causer. As time goes on, however, it can cause problems including depression. When you use techniques to release stress, you reduce the risk of having depression.

Improve Your Sleep Hygiene

Sleep and mood are intimately related, and depressed people experience sleep disturbances. If you feel like you can't fall asleep or struggle to get out of bed because of exhaustion all the time, then you should practice good sleep hygiene.

Improve Your Eating Habits

Researchers keep reiterating on the links between diet and mental health. Improving nutrition can prevent and treat mental illness. There are quite several brain essential nutrients that affect depression. So, if you want to find relief, you should improve your diet and speak with your physician on taking nutritional supplements.

Self Confidence and Self Esteem

Self-esteem is a term used to describe a person's overall sense of self-worth or personal value.

Self-esteem is basically how an individual feels about himself. How do you see yourself as a person? In what light do you portray yourself? How do you talk about yourself? How much do you love yourself?

Self-confidence, however, although used interchangeably refers to how you feel about your abilities and can vary depending on the situation.

Sometimes, one is forced to believe that self-esteem is formed based on a person's self-confidence in several activities. Let's say; you have the confidence to perform beautifully in several areas of your life; it makes you increase how much you love and value yourself. If you also love yourself very much, then your confidence can also grow.

The two terms have a relationship but do not always go hand in hand. Like it is possible to be highly self-confident and yet to have profoundly low self-esteem.

A self-confident person is ready to rise to new challenges, seize opportunities, deal with stressful situations, and take responsibility if and when things go awry. Self-esteem plays a very significant role in your motivation and success throughout your entire life.

People with healthy self-esteem do not need to prop themselves up with externals such as income, status, or notoriety, or lean on crutches such as alcohol, drugs, or sex. To the contrary, they treat themselves with the utmost respect and take care of their health, their community, and the environment. They can invest themselves completely in projects and people because they do not have a fear of failure or rejection. Even when they suffer hurt and disappointment, they do not allow their setbacks to either damage or diminish them.

Self-esteem and Social Anxiety Disorder

Self-esteem has been known to play a role in social anxiety disorder. A lowered self-esteem may put a person at risk of developing a social anxiety disorder. Also, having social anxiety may make a person feel worse about himself. The two afflictions interact to form a negative cycle.

Those who live with a social anxiety disorder may tell themselves that they cannot control their anxiety around people, so much until that's the only thing they believe about themselves. Such beliefs only help to increase anxiety and are usually based on low self-esteem.

People with low self-esteem usually have unrealistic social standards and trouble choosing achievable goals. For instance, you may believe that everyone must like you and then you have a morbid fear of doing or saying the wrong thing.

When faced with social situations that are quite challenging, you shift your attention inward towards your anxiety, view yourself negatively, and blow up the negative consequences of making mistakes.

Then you fall back to your former strategies, avoiding people, situations and using safety behaviors. You keep replaying all the things you feel you did wrong over and over.

With this attitude, social anxiety and low self-esteem keep interacting with each other and fueling each other in a vicious cycle.

You may feel safer staying away from an event or party or work meeting, but how does it make you think about you as a person? Think!

How A person Develops Low Self-esteem

Low self-esteem does not just happen overnight. It builds gradually over the years, and people with it may or may not have a good idea when they first started feeling such a way. Different factors influence one's self-esteem. Genetic factors that help shape the overall personality play a role. If you continuously receive a negative assessment from those around you are like to have low self-esteem issues. Additionally, your age, inner thinking, any potential illnesses, disabilities or even your job may affect your self-esteem.

- Criticism from parents
- Physical, emotional or sexual abuse
- Neglect or being ignored
- Teasing or bullying
- Ridicule by peers
- High standards and unrealistic expectations set by others

The above events can lead to lowered self-esteem when they occur early or late in life.

Symptoms that Show that you lack self-esteem

You Apologize For Living

What is your reaction if someone bumps into you on the street? Do you apologize? People with low self-esteem often have a distorted self-image and a not so accurate view of their worth. According to research, they genuinely feel like when things go wrong, it is somehow their fault.

You claim everything is luck.

How do you feel when something great happens to you? Do you say you were lucky to be in the right place at the right time? Most people with low self-esteem usually claim that they don't know why it happened because they're not worthy, even when these people worked their way to get to where they are.

You Buy Things You Don't Actually Like

When you shop for things, do you do so with the opinions of others in mind? On a more critical note, did you pick a major that you felt would impress your parents instead of the one to advance your dreams? Do you compare yourself to others a lot?

You hide in your room

Would you rather die than live with a roommate who is mad at you? Do you always worry about others being mad at you while your feelings about the same situation as well? Avoiding conflicts or saying things to please people is considered a sign of low self-esteem.

You have a weird habit

Maybe you bite the skin around your nails, pick at scabs or detach your body for hairs that you can pluck. This habit is called compulsive self-mutilation, and it is a common habit of people with anxiety or low self-esteem. They usually use it as a coping mechanism in uncomfortable situations.

You're always checking your phone for nonexistent messages

When there is a drop in the conversation, or you're left alone for a moment at a party, do you fish out your phone instead of chatting or mingling? You may be bored, or you're not confident enough to think that other people want to talk to you or will care about what you have to say. Poor social skills are signs of low self-esteem.

You tell dumb lies

You might be trying to keep the peace, or maybe you don't think the truth is worth hearing, but you tell little white lies all the time. When confronted, you might deny ever saying that. People with self-esteem issues usually wear masks or pretend to be something they're not just to gain approval.

How To Build Your Self Esteem

People usually find it easier to build their self-confidence than their self-esteem, and, conflating one with the other, wind up with a long list of perfect abilities and achievements. Rather than standing up to their imperfections and failures, they hide them behind their certificates and prizes or laurels they got for their accomplishments.

Benefits Of Having a High Self-esteem

You can be Yourself

Friends, family and loved ones may try to shape your life. High self-esteem makes you observe what they recommend, suggest or even try to impose on you without bending to their will. Because you watch, you're always open-minded and prepared to learn, but when it comes to decision making, you make decisions based on what's best for you. You do not force yourself to adapt your views, values or behavior to meet the expectations of others.

You accept disagreement

Everyone has an opinion about almost everything in life. Opinions matter because you could never get all the information you need on your own. Many important decisions you will make in life will depend on views. With high self-esteem, you're able to cope with setbacks because you believe that you did your best.

High self-esteem allows you to cope with others' disagreement because you understand that everyone has the right to their own opinion and will often disagree with you. Therefore, you don't feel worried about a dispute, you accept and move on.

You can articulate your views when challenged

You can know somebody's self-esteem just by challenging their opinions. A person with low self-esteem may get anxious when his beliefs or actions are challenged. Those with low self-esteem usually adopt people's view, and they back down when being challenged because of their inability to defend it. Because they do not even understand it, they struggle to protect it. Also if it's theirs, they may defer to your own opinion so that they won't upset you.

High self-esteem allows you to acknowledge the challenge and put your argument across without conceding or, the fear of disapproval. With self-confidence, you can defend your opinion. It doesn't mean that you will always convince others that you're right. It also doesn't mean that you won't accept that you're wrong if the other person's argument is genuinely convincing, but you will be able to argue your case and articulate your view.

You accept new challenges

When faced with a problem which requires you to step out of your comfort zone, what is your reaction?

Do you view it as something you have never done before and may likely fail at? So, you withdraw from the challenge and stay within your comfort zone.

Do you understand that you've not done it before, but see it as a fresh challenge and opportunity to learn even if things don't go your way?

The first view is the view of a person with low self-esteem while an individual with high self-esteem will adopt the second approach.

High self-esteem helps you understand that you need to grow and develop. To grow, you need to take on New challenges and push yourself to new levels. Even if you don't succeed at the first time of every new challenge, you realize that failure is temporary and the best learning opportunities come from setbacks and failures.

Therefore, when presented with an opportunity that requires stepping out of your comfort zone, you accept it with relish.

You do not fear uncertainty

Procrastination is usually caused by the need for certainty. Instead of acting on things need to do, you continue to out then off because you fear you won't do a perfect job.

With high self-esteem, you understand that perfection is neither possible nor necessary. Instead of wasting time, trying to work out the things you need to do to achieve a particular outcome you want; you identify what is required to do the best job you can. You then start working on the task to the best of your ability. You know that once you take action, you can get feedback which will allow you to improve on the job further.

When you have high self-esteem, you know that certainty and perfection cannot be achieved, and all work is a work in progress.

You do not need approval

Late Anthony De Mello said, "approval is the most dangerous drug in the world."

Humans would want to get along with other people and build relationships. There is nothing wrong with that as you need to cooperate with others to achieve far more than you ever could alone. But when you feel that you need others approval to validate you, you begin to sacrifice who you are.

When you have high self-esteem, you don't need to pretend to be something else to gain the approval of others. You have your approval and even though you hope that others will like you; you are determined to be yourself.

You understand that you cannot please everyone, so you do what you believe to be right. If people like you or not, you're unbothered, and you will maintain your high self-esteem.

It's ok not to know everything

Nobody wants to look stupid. And as you grow older, you will discover that the tendency of somebody being stupid is not so realistic. There is so much to know in the world, and nobody could ever know it all. And because we have different interests, our intelligence develops in different areas.

With high self-esteem, you realize that you can't possibly know everything and there is no use in pretending that you do. You will focus on what is essential and passionate to you without feeling bad that you do not know the answer to someone's question.

You can. Yes, you can! (Proactivity)

Proactivity means taking action in anticipation of a future situation instead if reacting. It entails taking control and making things happen other than adjusting to situations or just waiting for something to happen.

If you have a social anxiety disorder, that might be a little difficult for you as you're usually anxious, because you probably listen to your opinion about you which is low, hence the anxiety.

You already know that focusing internally on your anxiety thoughts and beliefs only exacerbate your problem; therefore, you should focus externally, on other people and the physical task around you.

Paying attention to your inner feelings usually brings problems and leads to defeat. Because focusing on your anxiety leads to more stress, you should turn your attention away from it.

Rather than always responding to life's events, you can act first. Be proactive. By doing that, you will feel better about yourself, your self-esteem will increase, and you begin to gain more confidence.

Let's say you decide to take the initiative and act first; for example; you greet a neighbor first. Because you did it first, you will feel less anxious and have more confidence. Instead of hiding and only responding to actions, you can avoid depression by doing things.

You might feel scared to do it, but the more you listen to other people "actively" by focusing on them, you will be able to hear them correctly and converse with them better. Your conversations will begin to flow and don't say you can't do it because you can.

There are three features of proactive behavior:

1. It is anticipatory - this has to do with acting in advance of a future event, instead of just waiting for it to happen and then, reacting.

2. It is change-oriented - proactivity involves taking control and causing things to happen. Not only adapting to a situation or waiting for it to arrive before you do anything.

3. It is self-initiated - It doesn't require asking an individual to act, and no detailed instructions are given before a person makes a move. It is independent.

How to identify pro-active people

-They know themselves.

Proactivity hints on self-knowledge. It means that an individual is aware and conscious and is in charge of decisions. Being proactive does not mean being "blindly active," but seeing oneself and weighing the limitations and possibilities that are available.

What qualities differentiate you from others? How do you improve? Have you identified your weaknesses at a personal or professional level?

Proactive people ask themselves these questions so they can fully understand themselves and their position to have greater confidence in their possibilities.

-They have self-confidence.

One character that leads to the dynamic attitude that proactive people show is that they have a storehouse if self-confidence. They reflect, plan and, act only when they are convinced that they are doing things right. This way, their self-esteem increases.

-They are creative and look for different solutions.

A proactive person finds it difficult to give up easily. When a standard solution does not have results, they search for a new alternative.

-They express Positivity

Proactive people always positively represent themselves; they have a proactive attitude.

Because proactive people are always seeking solutions to encounters, they try to achieve their goal and make use of positive language to open closed doors and push their way to get their goal. When you're optimistic, you'll see people seeking the solutions too.

-They think beyond the short term.

It is an exceptional quality of proactive people. A lot of individuals focus on their immediate tasks without really noticing the medium and long term changes going on. An active person needs to look forward to future needs and problems. Proactivity is an essential factor for leadership positions.

A proactive person tries to anticipate future needs and problems: these people know how important planning can be. Therefore, proactivity is very important for leadership positions.

-They have self-control

Proactive people are aware of the need to detach and avoid emotions when they are faced with finding solutions to problems. In situations when you're not in the best mood, being proactive is a plus. Proactive people have mastered how to put a position under control and calm those around them by showing respect for their opinions and their way of thinking.

-They are focused.

Proactive people always want to be active, so they do not have the time for unnecessary details. They reserve frivolous talks and activities until they are done with their tasks.

-They are constant.

Their self-confidence is their guide. Proactive people always plan, and with these two qualities, they know they are on the right track. Therefore they understand that it is necessary to wait a while longer before their results. They rarely give up easily.

– They are disciplined.

Discipline is one of the effects of productivity. When a person concentrates, then he knows what's coming next, is constant, is active and possesses self-control.

– They are persuasive.

Most people are not able to resist the awesomeness of a proactive person. They know how to persuade people because of their self-confidence, self-control, and ability to show respect for the ideas of others.

– They are sociable.

A proactive person with self-esteem, creativity, and positivity is usually very content in their social relationships.

-They learn from criticism.

Proactive people handle criticism better than others. Criticism for them means an opportunity to learn and improve. They learn from it instead of taking it personally.

-They are flexible.

Remember: proactive people are creative and want solutions to problems. They are more flexible and able to adapt well to situations.

How to be Proactive

If you take the initiative, say hello first, and start small conversations early, then you will feel more in control and better about yourself.

1. Predict

You need to develop foresight to be proactive.

To be proactive, you must first develop foresight. Learn to predict future occurrences. Proactive people are seldom caught by surprise. They anticipate problems and events. They understand how things work by looking for patterns, recognizing that regular routines and daily practices that exist daily.

In the course of such action, try not to allow yourself to become too complacent. You can use the past and your imagination to anticipate future outcomes. Don't rely only on the past to be the accurate predictor for the future. Make use of creativity and logic so that you can create several scenarios for how events will turn out.

2. Prevent

Because of their ability to predict, proactive people can foresee potential obstacles and make use of their power to seek ways of overcoming them before the simple constraints change into significant challenges.

They try to prevent problems that others might tag unavoidable. You should not allow yourself to be overcome by powerlessness. When faced with challenges, take control and face them immediately before they increase and grow into fatal problems.

3. Plan

Proactive people have ideas. To be like them, stay away from "here and now" thinking and make concrete plans and anticipate long-term consequences. You should try to create a rosy bridge between your present and future. Before making decisions, understand that every decision is linked to a series of events and other decisions before finally connecting to the conclusion. To make the right decisions, you how to know what you want to do and what you were before and where you want to end up.

4. Participate

Proactive people are not backseat observers; they are drivers' seat participants. To be proactive, you must learn to get involved. You should take initiatives, steps and be a part of a solution.

Do not be afraid to participate. Every human is only a piece of the whole, and we influence and are influenced by the actions of others. Don't merely react to the activities around you. Engage with them. Exercise your influence and put in your contribution.

5. Perform

Do things. Take timely and practical actions. That is the meaning of proactivity.

You must always be decisive and willing to do your work NOW. Procrastination is a deadly option and should be eradicated. Take command of your performance and hold yourself accountable. Always back your decisions.

Being proactive implies that you have adequately articulated and have decided to take careful, thoughtful steps to choose the appropriate path which means you're not just reacting impulsively to your environment.

How Proactivity helps reduce your social Anxiety

If you're socially anxious, then you may be wondering why and how the long talk on proactivity will help to reduce your social anxiety. Some people hide their social anxiety under the bogus claim on being introverted. If you acknowledge your disorder and you're willing to make changes, then proactivity is one of the traits you must affiliate with.

A study conducted by researchers showed that being proactive, optimistic and hopeful are traits associated with protecting so individual against negative emotions.

They also found out later brain volume in the areas that control these traits. A Maryland Psychologist Mary Karapetian Alvord said that the findings are in line with the idea that human thoughts are connected to physiology, which is connected to emotions, which are also linked to behavior.

Alvord, the clinical fellow to the Anxiety and Depression Association of America and an adjunct associate professor of psychiatry and behavioral sciences at the George Washington University School of Medicine and Health Sciences, says, "If you change your thoughts redeemed something from a different angle, it helps guard against your anxiety. It has also been validated by research to improve depression."

Benefits of being proactive

1. Acting proactively instead of reacting will not only cushion most situations and make it easier to navigate, but it will also guide you as you plan for your long-term goals. It is because you will start thinking about the consequences of actions even before the situations occur.

You'll also have more flexibility by thinking about the "what if's" early because you've been able to analyze and choose the best option or resolution on time instead of being coerced to do something at the last minute which might even turn out to be your last option.

Proactive people are generally more relaxed, prepared, and positive due to the preventive steps that they've taken for potential "situations." They are in control of their future.

2. Being proactive will make you more prepared for situations – You're thinking about what could happen today to avoid chaos in future, sort of like an insurance plan! You have set your succession and back up plan in place just in case the present situation did not work out for you.

3. Saves time and money – You're doing the work and putting in effort presently to save time and money by preparing for the unexpected problems now instead of at the last minute.

Recovering lost time is a Chief benefit of being proactive. As you start to can't you reactive mind, you been to understand that time was never the problem. You will come to realize that by being proactive you have a lot of time on your hands.

4. By being proactive, you alleviate problems or issues before they occur– You're able to discover the potential issues or conflict and reduce your exposure to it. For instance, there are specific environments or people that you are unable to stomach (negative people, biased critics, or "haters") so you avoid them or minimize your contact with these people or places.

5. It helps you to recognize a need for change – In the process of thinking ahead, you will come to see that there are things that you could change for the better. You could imagine yourself as a business owner in the future, and you begin to make the steps this moment to increase your skill set and to network with people already running such businesses.

6. It fosters creativity and change – Being proactive means that you're willing to step out of your comfort zone to make things work. Since you see the big picture, you will understand that certain things must be done now to ensure to keep to track with your long-term goals. In most cases, this means trying and doing something new. You may be a pub owner who has been running a cash-basis business, but to keep up with the needs of your clients and to keep up with the world of plastic (credit cards), you start to accept credit card payments via card readers (even on cell phones).

7. Allows for flexibility – Being proactive opens you to a world of options because you are considering things before they happen. You know what kind of business or activity you plan to start so you will begin to look for potential spaces in areas with demand for that your product or service.

8. Self-improvement and awareness – As you are now used to contemplating the "what if's," you can discover things about yourself that you've become accustomed to

unknowingly. If these habits are wrong, you will be encouraged to stop them, and if they are reasonable, you will keep working to improve them.

9. It makes you see the big picture and understand long-term goals – Acting proactively means that you are always looking forward. Your eating habits and exercise habits will be influenced and changed for the better. You're a representation of a positive change to your colleagues or employees and other people within your Empire.

10. More explicit directions for your future – if you're proactive, you don't include sitting back and waiting for things to happen in your to-do list. You know the path you've drawn for yourself, and you will stick to it. You know you're not at your desired position do you keep planning to go to the spot of interest. And it gives you peace of mind because you become happy with yourself and where you are going because you already have an idea of what is coming. It's more comfortable to sleep at night when there's a regular plan for the morning.

11. Authenticity

Most people claim to be active. But it is a different thing from proactivity. Proactivity is first and foremost a state of mind. The starting point is developing the freedom to act and not only to react. By reacting you are trapped in a repetitious and automated state of mind because you're being controlled by the habit of the moment.

But being proactive prevents your conscious intentions and desires from being pushed aside. You are encouraged to start living consciously and deliberately. You stay away from the conditioning and habits that have been taking shape in you for years, which have not been serving you well. You bring up an official version or you.

12. Presence of Mind

A reactive mind is always falling behind while life happens around and moves on. The reactive mind is busy, assessing and reacting trying to stay safe and alive.

This mechanism only helps in survival. It can quickly start working against the individual, and such a person loses connection to the present moment. Proactivity introduces consciousness and sanity to the reactive mind. It sets an individual into shape and balance and allows for the presence of mind to prevail.

Chapter Nine

Testimonies of winners

Listening and paying too much attention to your social anxieties would keep you from venturing out, from chasing the things you want to achieve. Fear of rejections and what that would mean to you could prevent you from being a winner. The critical attribute of a winner is falling and rising every time you fall. Dust off and head back into the challenge.

Below are stories of people who were seemingly failures, people who failed, not once, but failed countless times, but got up and headed back into their game. In the end, they won. They became celebrated and are still renowned today as no longer losers and failures, but winners. You too can.

Now that you already know that as humans, rejection is imminent and should be expected, I present to you real humans who have faced rejection and what they did to rise above rejection and how they succeeded in spite of rejection.

Don't get me wrong; I am not saying you should walk around life expecting and actively seeking rejection or be rejected. No! But instead, this will prepare you beforehand and help you deal with rejection anytime it comes.

So, join me as I take you through this journey of triumph.

J.ROWLING

"I've been writing since I was six. It is a compulsion, so I can't say where the desire came from; I have always had it. My first breakthrough with the first book came through persistence because a lot of publishers turned it down!"

-J.Rowling

If you are a fan of Harry Potter, then you should have heard about J.Rowling. No, we are not talking about Harry Potter even though I would love to talk about Dumbledore.

Born in the Southwest of England, Rowling grew up along the border of England and Wales with her father, mother, and sister. She had always known she would be a book author because, by her account, she had the perfect temperament for a writer and is perfectly happy alone in a room, making things up. Rowling wrote her first book at age six about a rabbit named Rabbit.

As humans, we have experienced events that left us traumatized, and for Rowling, her traumatizing event was the day her mother died, she was twenty-five years old at that time and six months after she began writing "Harry Potter." It was a painful experience because her mother never knew she was writing a book. The loss of her mother was what led her to make innocent Harry Potter suffer the death of his parents. It explains why her books are mainly about death and Voldemort's obsession with immortality and why he wants to conquer death.

The joy of every writer is to see their manuscript accepted and become published authors. So you can imagine the pain in J.Rowling's heart when she got loads of rejection from various book publishers when she first sent out her "Harry Potter and the Philosopher's Stone" manuscript.

She pushed and pitched and wrote until in 1997 Bloomsbury accepted and paid 2,500 for the manuscript. Her editor suggested she gets a teaching job since she was unlikely to earn a living from children's books. Interesting to note that three days after the "Harry Potter" book was published in the UK, Scholastic bid $100,000 for the American publishing rights, an unprecedented amount for a children's book at the time.

She eventually became the first person on earth to make $1 billion from writing books on earth. Yes, you read that right. The first person on earth to make a whopping $1 billion from writing books and her Harry Potter series has now sold more than 450 million copies, won countless awards, been made into movies, and transformed Rowling's life.

Maybe we should pause and drink some water at this point.

Alright, let's continue.

What was her motivation and what kept her going?

J.Rowling tweeted "I wasn't going to give up until every single publisher turned me down, but I often feared that would happen."

That was her motivation. She was willing to be turned down by every single publisher.

How determined can you be to be ready to face rejection by every single publisher on earth before giving up? Maybe you are not publishing a book, but how many times are you willing to be turned down before you finally give up?

How many times have you been rejected that you already say it is time to throw in the towel and kiss the feet of defeat?

Listen, if J.Rowling can do it; know that you can, you will, you must, and you have not to give up.

W.DISNEY

"All the adversity I've had in my life, all my troubles and obstacles have strengthened me... You may not realize it when it happens, but a kick in the teeth may be the best thing in the world for you."

W.Disney

Born in Chicago, and raised in Missouri, Disney was the fourth son among five siblings. Disney always found solace in drawing as a means of escape from his circumstances. He ran away from home and lied about his age to become an ambulance driver during World War 1. He became an apprentice at a Kansas City commercial art studio and itching to start his own, he and his older brother launched their own cartoon business in 1920 which went bankrupt a couple of years later.

He later moved on to Los Angeles with a bag of dreams and $40 to his name to try out acting which he failed at. He first succeeded with the creation of Oswald the Lucky Rabbit which his producer took all legal rights of ownership from him. He walked away after that and on the train ride back to California, he created Mickey Mouse.

A newspaper editor fired Disney for not being creative enough at age 22; this was enough to crush his dreams even before he started to pursue them. But because he was sold on his idea and he had faith in what he sees, he stayed on course and persevered through. In 1996, Disney bought the very newspaper that fired him for lacking creativity and, built it into an empire.

Success is indeed the best revenge you can serve.

Mickey Mouse, Aladdin, The Lion King, Beauty and The Beast and Frozen, to mention a few would not have existed if only Disney had cowered in the face of rejection.

What would you do if you kept going to a place and for every attempt; all you get is a deafening "NO"?

Disney's idea of Mickey Mouse was rejected 300 times because they thought the idea was absurd. Did you know that already?

Was the idea good enough? Yes

Was it a great idea? Well, the appearance, it was and is.

So why was it rejected 300 times and called absurd?

It is simple, in life; people will not always see things from your perspective. And since people will not ever see things from your perspective, it is up to you to hold on to what you are seeing and not relent or give up on your vision.

Think about Disney for a second and how it would have been like for him going through all those rejections. His friends, his family, the people around him. Imagine them telling him to forget about Mickey Mouse for his good and find something worthwhile doing. Imagine he had listened to them and thought to himself "well, they are right. This idea is absurd," and he dumped the entire Mickey Mouse into the trashcan of his mind; Disney World wouldn't have existed and the Disney Company, a global media and entertainment empire wouldn't have been born.

The creator of Mickey Mouse has been nominated for 59 Academy Awards of which he won 32 for his unparalleled animations. He still holds the records for the most Oscars won by an individual.

What made him different?

Walt Disney was a man with a clear vision, and he had faith in that vision sandwiched between slices of persistence with a glass of self-belief in himself just enough to give him the strength to keep him going.

Before you give up because the world has said you lack creativity and your ideas are absurd, think about Walt Disney and hang on.

OPRAH W.

"Do the one thing you think you cannot do. Fail at it. Try again. Do better the second time. The only people who never tumble close are those who never mount the high wire. This is your moment. Own it."

-Oprah W.

Oprah, yes the famous Oprah was born in a low-income family, and her parents who were not on good terms decided to be separated, and Oprah was sent to live with her grandmother. She was later sent back to her mother who gave her little attention. Her parents ignored her, and she felt so unloved she found love and calm in the arms of drugs. Again, she was sent to live with her father who thought he was strict, helped her get over her drug addiction and focus on her future.

Oprah got a job as a news reporter, but she was fired and told she is not fit for TV.

If you've seen Oprah on TV a lot of times, you might find this funny and want to laugh. Please do take some seconds to laugh. I'll wait.

Right! Let's get back to business.

It is quite interesting to note that Oprah did not give up. She might have been hurt, yes because she is human.

But give up? No, she didn't.

What happened next?

She was later invited to host a half an hour talk show that wasn't so popular, and within one year, that talk show became much more popular it was extended to an hour. The show was later called "Oprah W. show," and Oprah rose to become the No.1 talk show hosts and one of the most popular TV icons.

Yeah, you can say that again, "Somebody lied."

Have you been rejected?

Please smile and walk away and don't stop moving for if you do not stop, you'll prove those who rejected you wrong.

But an expert said;

So what? Who cares about what an expert said? Listen, in the grand scheme of things, and as it concerns your dreams and life, expert opinion do not matter only because experts are humans and again, they might fail to see your vision or understand your plan. Listen to an expert but don't take their opinion to heart. It is all about you.

Follow your dreams and don't be limited by anything and anybody, including an expert.

If Oprah can, you will too.

M. JORDAN

"I have missed more than 9000 shots in my career. I've lost almost 300 games. 26 times I have been trusted to take the game winning shot and missed. I have failed over and over and over again in my life. And that is why I succeed."

M. Jordan.

You probably must have heard the story of how Jordan did not make his high school team a million times already. Here it one more time and pay attention to the lessons in the story.

1978, M. Jordan tried out for the varsity basketball team at Laney High School. When the list was posted, his name wasn't on the list and instead he was asked to play on the junior varsity team. Now, the reason wasn't that Jordan didn't have enough talent or hadn't already distinguished himself as an outstanding basketball player but because of size, seniority and a strategic decision.

15-year-old Jordan was shattered when he saw the list without his name. In his mind, it was the ultimate defeat, the ultimate failure. In his words, "I went to my room, closed the door, and I cried. For a while, I couldn't stop. Even though there was no one else at home at the time, I kept the door shut. It was important to me that no one hears or sees me."

He was ready to give up the sport altogether until his mother convinced him otherwise.

In life, there will always be that one person to cheer you up, get you back on your feet and or believes too much in you to allow you and your dreams go to waste. Find that one person. And if you already have, make sure you do not lose them.

Jordan picked himself up and used failure and disappointment as the drive to be better. He played on the team and worked himself to the limit.

"Whenever I was working out and got tired and figured I ought to stop, I'd close my eyes and see that list in the locker room without my name on it, and that usually got me going again."

It happened such that in Jordan's life, a disappointment or setback resulted in a redoubling of effort.

For a lot of people, public rejection results in public humiliation and withdrawal from the public. For example, a lot of people are afraid of speaking in general and about 75% of the world's population experience some degree of anxiety around public speaking. Your fears have little to do with speaking and far more to do with the perceived impact and reaction that your audience may have. Jordan transformed the fear of failure and ridicule into a drive for success. His relentless drive would lead him to break numerous records and become the world's most decorated player in the history of the NBA.

He's credited with increasing the popularity of basketball both in the United States and internationally, and he is an inspiration to L.James, D.Wade, and K.Bryant.

You can't define the word "champion" without Michael Jordan in it, and when next you need to prove that failure is a stepping stone to success, Michael Jordan is your best proof.

A.EINSTEIN

"Out of clutter, find simplicity."

"From discord, find harmony."

"In the middle of difficulty lies opportunity."

A.Einstein

Einstein is another name for the genius because this guy was a genius in the genuine sense of fact. But his success story didn't happen overnight. He had to jump hurdles, and he overcame difficulties before he became known for what he is known for today.

Einstein didn't speak until three years of age, and it took him several more years before he could speak fluently, he couldn't even read till he was seven and elementary school was a struggle for him and a lot of people suspected him to be a retard, and people believed he would never succeed at anything. After he graduated from college, he worked in a patent office as a clerk because the job was mostly mindless and afforded him the free time to study and research scientific theories he was working on.

Regardless of Einstein's rejection and setback, he continued his studies and experimentation on his theories, and he was not recognized by the scientific community until he published his first theories – the theory of relativity. Even then, many scientists ridiculed him and attacked his theories calling them worthless but yet, Einstein went on to become a professor at the university in Zurich and later, professor of theoretical physics at Prague.

He proved to the entire doubting, ridiculing and demeaning scientists in the world that he did have a brilliant mind and was capable of success by winning the Noel Prize in Physics in 1921.

"Great spirits have always encountered violent opposition from mediocre minds. The mediocre mind is incapable of understanding the man who refuses to bow blindly to conventional prejudices and chooses instead to express his opinions courageously and honestly."

People contend and demean what they cannot understand. So when next people laugh at you or call you or your ideas a failure, when people say you cannot amount to anything in life, let A.Einstein be the motivation you need to succeed.

You are not a failure until you see yourself as a failure.

These are stories of famous people who have faced rejection at some point in their life, but they rose above it; used it as building blocks of success and triumph.

What about the stories of ordinary everyday people?

A friend of mine was once rejected at a job because according to the university, his grades and qualification were beneath the required standard of grades for lecturing job. He loves to teach and badly needs to get a job that affords him the pleasure of teaching and transferring knowledge. He applied over and over again, and he was told that with his grades, no one will ever employ him as a teacher.

He was so sad, and he cried for days till he looked in the mirror and said "I am not my grades. I have a lot to offer. My value is not tied to my grades. I am not my grades." That became his mantra, and he applied for a teaching job in another school, and he got the job. He saw that as a better opportunity to teach and in his words, "I didn't only teach those students, I tapped into the potentials and helped them become better than they were. It was an amazing experience. And as for the rejection due to my grades, I keep proving I am not my grade and even where I work currently, I keep working to improve myself and provide real value because I know what I am capable of and my value is not tied to my grade."

*

Do not allow anyone to put you down by their words.

When people tell you're not good enough, show them you're better than the best.

When they say you cannot amount to anything, laugh at them and show them you can be all that is in you to be.

When they say, you're not fit for a task, improve yourself and be the best person that can do that task.

When people reject you or your dreams, tell yourself it is the time to work on it and turn it into reality. Do not allow them project fears into you in the name of mentorship or friendship.

In conclusion, rejection does not have to mean you are not good enough; frequently, it means the other person failed to notice what you have to offer. Do not feel bad if someone rejects you or ignore you. People usually reject and ignore expensive thins because they cannot afford them.

When you are rejected, it is not always about you. Sometimes, it is about the other person.

Conclusion

In this age of social media and the internet, this age of social networks and media, everyone is on the internet, using the internet. Everyone is living or hiding their identities on the net. Here on our favorite social media and networks like Facebook, Instagram, Twitter, people suffering from social anxiety disorders are made to appear and look proactive to the world, like everyone else. To chat with ease, create networks too and have fun.

While social media has its huge perks, people suffering from social anxiety disorders have used it as a way to hide from themselves, to pretend it is real and the only life there. They begin to think it is enough.

"I have 3,000 friends. I have 2,000 followers." But in the end, it is all online, all cyber, all imaginary and not real.

Online love and interactions are not enough. You have to seek out tangible things too. You have tried to reach out, connect and interact with the realities around you, with real people and real friends. Your smartphone, your social media is to be utilized into creating an authentic, sustainable bond and connections. Use it to find the world, then drop it and interact with the world, and continue the circle. And for this to be done, we have to ask ourselves some question, understand some specific things and follow a laid out strategy to achieving this.

Questions like: How can someone suffering from social anxiety use social media as a tool to heal themselves and enhance their interactions with others? Well, let's understand certain things first.

– Social Media was not designed as a tool for escape or to patronize our introversion; they are not meant to shield us from the reality we live in. On the contrary, social media were created as a means of networking and interaction with reality. They were designed to broaden our scope and reach.

– Alone, without social media, there is only so much we can achieve and meet. But the advent of social media had given us a larger platform for our interaction, a bigger sphere to walk and communicate with. Now, we are not limited to having friends from our neighborhood, or our school. Now we can walk to other areas, and school and places meet people.

– As a person suffering from social disorders and fear of social settings, the use of social media platforms is an excellent thing, not for hiding, but exposure. You can chat, you can hold conversation virtually. If you can do that practically, you sure can do it in reality. You have to believe that, there are no two ways about that.

Chat up, people. It is what you do already. Create a good personality for yourself, not hiding your real nature. You can only be Yourself because every other person is taken. Get to know people and let them know and meet you. Talk about hobbies, about your interests, talk about trends and news. Have dissenting views and come to a

mutual understanding. This way you are slowly creating
a connection.

Thanks for reading,

Clark Brown